And Still They Come...

Edited by Bill Rhatican

authorHOUSE

1663 LIBERTY DRIVE, SUITE 200
BLOOMINGTON, INDIANA 47403
(800) 839-8640
www.authorhouse.com

First published by AuthorHouse 06/02/04

ISBN: 1-4184-7676-5 (e)
ISBN: 1-4184-7677-3 (sc)

Library of Congress Control Number: 2004093493

Printed in the United States of America
Bloomington, Indiana

This book is printed on acid-free paper.

Preamble

Welcome to a wonderful world of people who, experiencing severe hardships in their own communities, make the heart-wrenching decision to leave their homelands and travel thousands of miles towards a dream – of political liberty, religious freedom or simply better economic opportunities for themselves and for their children.

The essays you are hopefully about to enjoy are all written by high school seniors as part of their Advanced Placement US Government class at West Potomac High School, Alexandria, Virginia. As their teacher, I gave them the assignment to research and write an essay about an immigration group of their choice, detailing the hopes, dreams and aspirations as well as the realities of their journies to the "Promised Land."

What they produced lies within the following pages. They covered many continents and countries in their research and writing and presented a panoply of viewpoints. One perspective comes from Kwadwo Danquah, himself an African immigrant who still embraces the American dream in spite of the realities he faces here.

At the other end of the spectrum are the views of Phil John, Kim Wagner and Ahren Freund who adopt the Nativist view that the traditional northern European values on which this country was founded are being lost through immigration. Another essay, by Kara Hardie, identifies the

Nativist response to the mid-19th century Irish immigration as "a proper response to the invasion of a foreign group of people…from a country engulfed in disease, starvation, and dictatorship."

Whatever your personal political beliefs – and I have my own – I think these young people rather accurately reflect the perpetual American dilemma: whom to let in, from where, why and how many is enough. They have contributed to the debate in a very definitive, positive way. I am proud to have been associated with each essay and every student behind it. I want to especially thank Sabrina Buckley for her tireless efforts to make this project successfully. Without her pushing and prodding it never would have happened on time.

William F. Rhatican
December 2003

Introduction

Did the American Revolution end with the Treaty of Paris in September 1783 or is it still raging, ever broadening its scope and depth to include those originally excluded from its mandate and, indeed, those who were not even born in or near the new nation when it was formed? The entire question of freedom and its various interpretations springs among us again, especially in the wake of the dastardly attack on the United States on September 11, 2001, causing those who feel threatened by all new arrivals to question whether any new arrivals should be allowed.

Intertwined with the natural anguish created by the September 11 attack is a deeper tension between those who have been here for some time and those who seek what we have and are willing to pay any price to achieve the American dream, however one interprets that dream. As David Sidorsky so aptly phrased it in the Partisan Review, "Interpretations of freedom have been perennially contested and are continuously changing...even though the idea of freedom has been constant as a rhetorical idea for human aspirations and as a source of social values."

The many definitions of freedom are altered based on the perspectives of the individuals and/or groups espousing freedom for themselves, a tension that predates the American Revolution itself and follows a twisting and sometimes tortuous road through the American experience to its current manifestation of what might be called the "Drawbridge mentality," that is, pull up the drawbridge now that I am here and don't let anyone else in.

For example, newspaper columnist and former Presidential candidate Pat Buchanan has written that "Uncontrolled immigration threatens to deconstruct the nation we grew up in and convert America into a conglomeration of peoples with almost nothing in common – not history, heroes, language, culture, faith, or ancestors, Balkanization beckons." When he wrote those words, he sounded much like Pierce Butler of South Carolina during the Constitutional Convention who wrote, "They (foreigners) bring with them…ideas of Govt. so distinct from ours that in every point of view they are dangerous."

Pat Buchanan is just as wrong today as Butler was more than 250 years ago and for many of the same reasons. Although I count Buchanan as a friend, a former colleague in the Nixon White House and a fellow-offspring of Irish immigrants, Pat should be expected to be somewhat more amenable to immigration today than were the white Anglo-Saxon Protestants who populated the United States when his family (and mine) sought refuge here with their strange language, religion, customs and Old World loyalties. The Nativist arguments of today's Buchanans, however, are unlike the arguments of earlier generations in that the earlier Nativists feared only the immigrant. Today's Nativists fear comes in equal parts of basic Nativist distrust of the new arrivals and fear of the United States governmental establishment, which, unlike the establishment of the 1850s, has a tendency to ameliorate the plight of today's immigrant with little or no input from the immigrant himself.

Essentially, what today's establishment is saying – and what Buchanan and his followers are objecting to – is that today's immigrant, unlike virtually all of his predecessors in American history, is unable to take care of himself and become "Americanized" without the massive, heavy hand of governmental agencies and their non-governmental allies. In other words, the American bureaucracy and its allies in academia and the media are denigrating the immigrant, de-humanizing him and creating an atmosphere in which the immigrant today cannot succeed on his own and may achieve a modicum of "success" only with the help of the establishment. Thus, California's "multi-cultural" and multi-lingual educational system fosters the status quo of a perpetual underbelly class of immigrants who are prevented from becoming "Americanized" by the very establishment that should be encouraging them to participate fully within the American system, including the ability to fail.

Cooler, and wiser, heads prevailed at the Constitutional Convention including George Washington, who wrote of new immigrants, "the tide of population and wealth would flow to us, from every part of the Globe, and…make us the happiest people on earth." And, one may assume, cooler and wiser heads will also overcome this latest attack of Nativism, a viral infection that reappears periodically on the body politic.

What the reader is about to enter is a series of essays written by Advanced Placement United States Government students at West Potomac High School in Fairfax County, Virginia. The essays were an assignment, in which the students were allowed to select any immigrant group they chose and report on what they found. In some cases, the reader will discover immigrant groups who entered the United States "under the radar" of the national media, such the "56ers," the Hungarian Freedom Fighters. In others, the reports will be about familiar immigrants – the Italians and Irish. In still others, the reader will learn new and interesting information about immigrant groups and how they assimilated without the assistance of the federal government. The reader may also discover that the American government was much more conciliatory to immigrants who were escaping Communist regimes, such as those in Cuba and Hungary but much less receptive to immigrants from our "client states" such as El Salvador.

Every essay is student-written and only mildly edited for consistency. The words are the students' own. The thoughts are theirs, including one essay that suggests, as Buchanan does, that American society is undergoing a permanent and dramatic change from the America we all know and respect. With that assessment I agree. Where we disagree lies in the result of the current changes and what America will look like in the end. It is my view – perhaps best demonstrated by the diversity within the student body at our own high school – that each new group of immigrants brings with it a rich and vibrant cultural background that adds so much to the fabric of the American mosaic.

I am very proud of their work and their diligence in exploring a topic for which many of them had been unprepared and, frankly, unwilling at first. I believe the reader will see the development of certain subtle trends in our view of today's immigrants that mirrors an earlier, dark view by our ancestors as well as a sense of welcoming to those who are willing to abandon all they hold dear to achieve the "American dream."

There are certain undeniable themes that reoccur throughout this work as we look at each immigrant group: fear of the unknown, second thoughts after their arrival here; homesickness; resentment at the treatment they receive here and ultimate success in overcoming Nativist obstacles until they become truly Americanized. May the current immigrants and refugees recognize the pattern and, perhaps, break it on behalf of those to come later.

African Immigration
by Kwadwo Danquah

Every economically strong, well-populated country has minority groups. These minority groups consist of many different people from many different cultures. In America, these minority groups are obvious. America and other "well to do" countries attract many people from different countries. Their strong economies and strong political views make it possible for people of other nationalities to come here and seek refuge from political persecution and economic distress.

Most of the black people came from Africa, either through slavery or by their own "free will." The blacks who came here after slavery came for their own individual reasons. Some came here due to political instabilities in their own countries, while others came for economic "salvation." All these individuals with their distinctive reasons came together to form the black minority of the United States. These immigrations first started with students winning scholarships for an education here. They soon realized the way of life in this country was much better than those of their native countries and stayed, encouraging others to begin to migrate to this country.

What distinguishes this century's immigration from Africa to America from that of earlier centuries, is that it was not the result of forced removal from Africa, but rather a voluntary decision made by the Africans seeking "greener pastures." Since the end of forced migration, however, only a small number of Africans have been able to come to the United States in contrast with other immigrant groups.

From 1820 to 1993, America only took in 418,000 African immigrants, according to Immigration and Naturalization (INS) records. Only in the last quarter of the century, has the number of African immigrants grown tremendously. Two-thirds of all African immigrants currently in the United States arrived after 1980. At the time of the 1990 census, African-born residents numbered 364,000 according to the 1990 Report on foreign-born residents in the U.S.

INS records show that in 1820 only one person emigrated from Africa to America. Sixteen more people came throughout the entire next decade. The number of African immigrants climbed slowly until the 1960s, when it began to grow rapidly. The reason for the small numbers of African immigrants is due to the difficulty in obtaining immigrant visas, except for a small number of students with bona fide acceptance to educational institutions in the U.S. and some political exiles from South Africa. Another reason for the small number of immigrants was the long, expensive journey that was beyond the reach of most African families.

African-born residents in the United States are highly educated and urbanized, having one of the highest per capita incomes of any immigrant group. An article in *The Economist* magazine in its May 11, 1996 issue stated, "...Three-quarters have some college experience; one in four has an advanced degree." These impressive figures even surpass the figures for native-born Americans. "Nearly 88 percent of adults who immigrate from Africa to the U.S. have a high school education or higher.

Nevertheless, they do not get any respect from most native-born Americans. They normally see an African immigrant as an uncivilized person with nothing better to do than to come here. Americans have always been critical of foreigners, which is understandable, but does not make sense seeing that all Americans here are all immigrants or descendants of immigrants. Even the first people who founded this country were immigrants who came from Europe, even though these groups do not see themselves as foreigners. They treat most immigrants, especially Africans, as though they were the filth of the earth. Anyway, immigration from Africa to this great nation has not lost its popularity in Africa. The racial discrimination in this country does not seem to deter most Africans. They see this nation as a place of great opportunities. They most often see this nation to be more than it really is. They come here with such great expectations that they tend to be disappointed when they realize that this nation has a lot to do with hard work. They sometimes want to return but they see that even though they work hard here, they get more for their hard work than in their native countries. Africans love this place because of the many liberties here. They love the many freedoms that make this nation so great.

Religion is a major part of African immigrants. The most popular religion amongst Africans is Christianity. This is obvious in the east coast, e.g. Maryland. When one sees all the churches in African communities, one can see that Christianity is one of the greater religions in Africa and one rarely sees Africans practicing their "traditional" religions. There are almost no Africans who continue with their traditional African religion when they arrive in the United States.

As already noted, African immigrants are putting the freedom of religion to good use. They do not accept all American values, including all of our freedoms. For example, Africans believe in keeping their children in check. They believe in punishing their children when they act in an unacceptable manner. This difference in child rearing has led to the American government to step in and "protect" these kids from their "abusive" parents. But Africans believe these checks are the cause of Africans not having as many problems with their young ones as Americans.

African immigrants publish newspapers and produce radio programs, the main purpose of which is to promote awareness of Africa among the African immigrants. The *'African Shopper'* is one of the newspapers widely circulated through African stores and other businesses in the Washington Metropolitan area and carries news items from Africa, opinion articles as well as poetry and stories. These news media help inform African immigrants in this nation about what is going on in their native countries.

Many believe the flow of African immigrants into this country will continue to increase until poverty in Africa is dramatically reduced. The American dream is famous in Africa. This dream is so accepted that Africans come here just to experience this dream.

Chinese Immigration in the 1800s: Was It Worth It?

by Amanda Price

A traditional and exclusive people, the Chinese were a world apart from Western Civilization. Western culture finally broke through the Chinese's self-imposed barrier with the selling of opium to the addicted Chinese and the following Opium War. The British victory in the War signaled the downfall of the Chinese empire and made the already harsh living conditions of the Chinese even worse. To escape from oppression, hard labor, poverty, and famine, the Chinese looked for a better place to live, and set their sights on America.

Unfortunately for the Chinese, America was not quite what they had dreamt it to be. Instead of living free in a beautiful country and finding gold in California, the Chinese were forced to work for low wages for those who paid for their passage to America. They were also held in camps for questioning and processing. The Chinese were held like prisoners waiting to be allowed into America at Angel Bay in San Francisco, the western coast counterpart of Ellis Island. They were also ridiculed for their Asian characteristics and different culture. These traits weren't even understood by other immigrant groups, who could not connect with the totally alien customs brought by the Chinese. This lack of understanding prevented the groups from accepting each others' differences and led to outright discrimination simply because the Chinese looked different from everyone else. To everyone else except another Chinaman, the Chinese were unacceptable and inferior.

To make matters even worse, the American government did little to help the Chinese and even hindered them. The Chinese could not vote, hold public office, or practice certain trades, but they could rightly be called the builders of America. They were the mass laborers who mined, farmed, and started businesses all across the western United States. They even built the first transcontinental railroad. Once the railroad was complete, all the Chinese laborers were laid off, leaving many people without jobs. Since California's economy was doing poorly at that time, others blamed the Chinese for taking their jobs, a familiar pattern with new immigrant groups. This is evident in a song sung to the tune of *The Wearin' o' the Green*, "*O, California's coming down, as you can plainly see. They are hiring all the Chinamen and discharging you and me.*"

Prejudice and high unemployment caused the Chinese to be very poorly treated. Their homes and businesses were destroyed, and no Chinese person could go outside without being beaten in the streets. Many Chinese were killed as victims of prejudice; no one was ever punished for committing these acts of violence. In addition to mistreatment by other people, the government also mistreated the Chinese by inserting parts of the manifesto of the Workingmen's Party (a political group that advocated "the Chinese must go") into the California state constitution. The Workingmen's Party's manifesto stated, "…before the world we declare that the Chinaman must leave our shores…death is preferable to life on a par with the Chinaman." The new state constitution proclaimed that companies and local governments could not hire Chinese workers, and enabled towns and cities to pass laws that would keep Chinese residents living in isolated neighborhoods.

Anti-Chinese feelings were only heightened by the fact that Chinese workers were quick to learn, worked for low wages, and did not go on strike often. The Chinese were believed to be inferior, dirty, savage heathens who did not believe in Christianity and lived in filthy slums. While the other unfair claims are untrue, the Chinese *did* live in slums of a sort. The Cubic Air Ordinance (1871) required that there must be at least 500 cubic feet of living space for each adult. Because there were so many Chinese in the isolated districts, there was no way that this rule could be maintained, landing many Chinese people in jail for breaking this ordinance (The jails eventually became so overcrowded with Chinese for breaking the ordinance that they accused the government of breaking it as well, and it was repealed). Finally, in 1882, the U.S. Congress passed the Chinese Exclusion Act, which barred the immigration of Chinese laborers for ten years.

It has been a long while since the Chinese attained full rights in the United States. The Chinese faced many hardships in the U.S. due to their distinct differences in culture and appearance, but they persevered to finally find their long-sought freedoms. Though the Chinese today, just as other groups, still face poverty and other forms of discrimination, many other Chinese have found, nay, carved, their own place in America, working hard to overcome the difficulties they found in facing people with different customs and narrow outlooks. The Chinese refused to give up their struggle and have endured. Though their chances of survival were next to nothing, leading to the phrase, "a Chinaman's chance," the Chinese people fought for and won their rights, becoming broadcasters, ice-skaters, architects, cellists, teachers, doctors, and senators. No one of Chinese descent has become President…yet. Mr. Yunian Zhang, the Chinese language teacher at West Potomac High School, says, "America is one of the best places to be. We just need to guard our liberty and freedom." Coming to America, though grueling, was definitely worth it in the long run. Though there are still more than a few kinks to work out in the American government and its immigration policies, it is evident that we have come a long way since the Chinese first came to the United States. It is just a work in progress.

Salvadoran Immigrants:
By Dany Hernandez

In order to understand the U.S. government's immigration policies and their effect on El Salvador's population, one first has to know a bit of background information about the country. Although El Salvador is the smallest Central American republic, it is second in population only to Guatemala and is the most densely populated nation in the Americas. The country has traditionally been rural, though it has seen significant migration toward its major cities in the last decades. It has also seen a lot of emigration due to the civil strife experienced in the 1980s. The United States often times intervened in order to prevent Marxist guerilla rebels from taking over the country during the Reagan and Carter administrations.

According to Encarta, El Salvador's population in 1992 was 5.2 million and is currently estimated to be about 6,470,379. The country has seen rapid growth in the 1900's, occasionally increasing more than 3 percent a year. A 2003 estimate puts the density of population in the area of 308 people per sq km (796 per sq mi). By comparison, in 1821 those numbers were only 12 people per sq km (31 per sq mi) and 38 per sq km (98 per sq mi) in 1900. The population growth rate has declined and currently stands at 1.8 percent. This is due to a decrease in birth rate, more common use of birth control and emigration. More than 1 million Salvadorans live outside the country and in 1995 about 6 of every 1,000 left to find better conditions abroad. El Salvador's large young population (38 percent under age 15) and its small population of elderly citizens (only 5 percent over age 65) have made for an attractive place for foreign companies to bring in their factories that require manual labor. One more thing to keep in mind is that its population is mostly Catholic. The country is ironically named El Salvador (the savior) in honor of Jesus Christ even though it is one of the most secular in Latin America. Birth control is used more than in most Central American countries which, as noted above, has caused a decline in its growth rate.

One of the defining characteristics of Salvadoran society is the polarization of money and land, the dramatic difference between the "haves" and "have-nots." Most of its population falls into the "have-nots" category, many of whom are mestizos (of European and Native American descent). Due to its large population and the small amount of land available, land has always played a vital role in its development. Its agriculture has broken or boosted its economy because of its dependence on just one or two products such as coffee or rice. Land has also been a subject of heated contention, within the country and as well as with other countries. There have been numerous coups in history and just about as many constitutions, 23 to be precise. Land disputes with other countries at times even resulted in war such as in the 1969 war with Honduras (sometimes referred to as the Soccer War). The shortage of land has also caused many to head north, mainly to the U.S. and Mexico.

During the 1980s up until today, a point of major debate for many is the United States' immigration laws. Estimates during the 1980s put the number of illegal Salvadorans in the U.S. at 500,000. A United States immigration law handed down in 1987 required illegal Salvadorans to be expelled if they came in after 1982, however, most of the illegal immigration took place after this period. The Salvadoran government worried about this because of the strain the deportation of those immigrants would place on the Salvadoran economy and services. Another reason was that, without the emigrants, there would be nobody to send money back home, estimated to be about $1.4 billion U.S. dollars per year. However, today that figure is estimated to be as high as $2 billion per year. In the '80s the Salvadoran government pleaded to keep those Salvadorans in the U.S. by having the White House grant them exemption from certain laws but the White House refused its plea. Legislation, though, held up their deportation as Congress considered bills to exempt Nicaraguans and Salvadorans.

Since the 1980s, some different rulings have allowed Salvadorans and other Central Americans to remain. Some of them included the temporary amnesty periods that were granted during the times of Hurricane Mitch and the earthquakes that hit the country in 2001. For the hurricane, the amnesty period for illegal immigrants from El Salvador and Guatemala expired on Monday, March 8, 1999.

My family has experienced the effects of all these actions by the government. My mother, Ana Elizabeth Hernandez, and my father, Jose Antonio Hernandez, first came to the U.S. in the late 1980s. Most of my family was here by that time. We (my siblings and I) came later in September of 1993. While here, dealing with INS (Immigration and Naturalization Service) was always burdensome and took a lot of time. The application process was lengthy and slow with numerous interviews on multiple occasions. When applying for our green cards, even though my mother already had hers, we had to wait for a few years. (My mom, by the way, had a work permit and later applied for her green card through her employer, which is a route commonly used by many non-green card holders). This demonstrates that while the process for filing papers for immediate family members for resident alien status is cumbersome for the applicants, it usually works. Preference is given to those who are resident aliens and have children or immediate family members. The process for getting a green card is further speeded up if one's spouse "happens" (wink, wink) to be an American citizen.

Marrying someone in order to become an American citizen, and not for love, is illegal. However, many people sometimes turn to this route in order to turn a profit. One such example would be a family friend, whom we shall call Lora, who married a girl just to get his papers. The sham is really hard to pull off but with enough determination and planning, it can (this is just one of the many weaknesses of the American immigration establishment by the way). They did not live together but during certain times INS agents would show up unannounced. They were interviewed and kept under close scrutiny. Lora, while he did manage to get his papers (only his green card), remained married to the girl for about 5 years. This was a really long time but what was in it for the girl? Well, she made some unknown thousands of dollars. Some people have taken advantage of laws such as these, and made the situation a very profitable one or two time business.

Most people do not file for their papers for fear that they might be rejected or, even worse, deported. Most Salvadorans, keep in mind, are deeply distrustful of government because of their native government's inability to take care of their country and allow them their freedoms, many of which are stated in the country's constitution. One more reason people do not apply is that they do not want to lose money. Just filing the applications is expensive; the application for a work permit costs about $100, plus the fee the notary charges. Applying for a green card is even more expensive. First, one has to hire a lawyer, who can charge thousands of dollars per case. Remember, too, that just because an application is filed, it does not guarantee approval. Some apply for their green cards more than once, wasting tens of thousands of dollars each time. Of course, this price depends on the lawyers and how good they are.

It is no surprise that many turn to illegal ways to acquire their papers. There is a large underground network of businesses that sell illegal immigrants their papers (from a social security card to a green card to even a passport). Some also pay thousands for these false documents. Most law-abiding immigrants, however, do not resort to this route because by doing so they might be destroying their chance to become legal green card holders or full-fledged U.S. citizens.

In this area, one need not go any farther than the Washington D.C. metropolitan area, especially near the Hispanic neighborhoods, to find people who sell counterfeit green cards. They are easy to spot, they might be standing on a street corner, usually wearing long, trench-like coats, very friendly-like, and they will blatantly ask if one wants one's papers (they only ask those whom they know are Hispanic). Law enforcement really has no chance to catch people like this because they are so elusive, they know whom to approach, when to approach, and are always on the lookout for the police. Of course, this is just general behavior I've observed from some of those who actually do this for a living (we used to be approached by people like this all the time in

Washington D.C. when we used to drive in my Dad's old, late 1980s, tan, Toyota van).

All these people, however, were reacting to the government's immigration laws in their own little ways. Not everyone can afford to do things the legal way, especially when they have so many people back home depending on them. One example of the hardworking immigrant, who does things the right way, is my aunt, Dora. Even though all her kids are in El Salvador, she works and sends them a couple hundred dollars every month. However, not all are as fortunate as she. Just go out to Four Mile Run area in Arlington, Virginia to see it. There one will see people actually just standing there ready to be picked to do any kind of job available by whomever.

However, despite whatever the circumstances an immigrant finds himself in, he should take the legal route. It is understandable though, that there are sometimes too many roadblocks before them, some of which are impassable.

Cuban Immigration

by Ahren Freund, Philip John, Kimberly Wagner

In 1959, while trying to battle communist tensions throughout the western hemisphere and with the American economy near its best, the United States government allowed for the entry of one million Cuban exiles into the country. Cuban immigration brought an entirely different class of immigrant to the United States; the first immigrants did not have any desire to assimilate into American society and never would. These Cuban immigrants set a high standard for themselves, which contributed to why "Cuban Americans have, as a whole, achieved greater success in a shorter time than any comparable immigrant group in the history of the United States."1 The United States experienced a tremendous shift in cultural identity as a record number of Cuban immigrants began to enter the United States as a result of the Great Migration.

In the early 1950s there were approximately 30,000 Cubans living the United States. This number increased by over 300 percent as the United States, especially Florida, became flooded with Cuban exiles and refugees. The United States government welcomed Cuban immigrants with somewhat open arms. They migrated to the United States mainly seeking refuge from Castro's oppressive, communist government. This communist government took full force on New Year's Day 1959, as Fidel Castro assumed power of a corrupt state, sending waves of people on their way to the United States.

Between 1902 and 1959, Cuba was ruled by a plethora of corrupt government officials. The foundation for a traumatic revolution was laid in 1952 when Fulgencio Batista illegally overthrew elected President Ramon Grau San Martin, and then went on to abuse his stolen power. In opposition to Batista's newly commandeered position, a revolution was developing as Castro assembled a trained guerilla group. This group was successful in overthrowing Batista, consequently gaining popular support from the oppressed Cuban people. As a result, Batista was forced to resign, leaving Castro and his revolutionaries in a powerful position. After developing his heroic image, Castro declared himself prime minister. The illusion of Castro's heroism was quickly proven false, as the promised democracy turned out to be the complete opposite, a communist dictatorship. The Cuban government implemented strict controls on all economic activity including seizing power over three oil refineries owned by American and British firms. Additionally, the government divided United States controlled sugar crops into state-run communes farmed by peasants. Castro even went so far as to abolish the freedom of press and to impose a G-2 Force (a police force whose sole purpose was to root out opposition to the government). Living in fear, Cubans had lost almost all freedom and it became an ongoing challenge to survive within the constraints of a dictatorship.

Cuban migration to the United States transpired in several waves, starting with the upper class and ending with the lower class. Each wave worked itself down the social hierarchy ladder. In 1959, immediately following the revolution, the Batistianos (Cubans associated with Batista) departed from Cuba.[2] This group was composed of upper class Cubans including business executives and sugar mill owners who profited from Batista's government. Not only did the Cuban government rob them of their property, but it also instilled fear of the changes being instituted.

The second wave occurred from April 1961 to October 1962, as the middle class fled from Cuba. The middle class became convinced after the United States-led invasion of the Bay of Pigs that there was no future for them in Cuba. To their dismay, the United States ended all military and financial support to the Cuban freedom fighters (anti-Castro organizations who fought for Cuban freedom) and began to prosecute them for violating the U.S. Neutrality Act by using weapons that the United States had given them.[3] The exiles began to feel that they were falling from the grace of the United States. They also became concerned for the fate of their children. It was rumored that their children might secretly be sent to the Soviet Union or that parents might lose the "patria potesda" (legal or moral rights that parents hold over their children).[4] Thousands of Cuban children between the ages of 6-16 were sent to the United States under the guardianship of the Catholic Church of Miami. An additional 14,000 children entered the United States through the "Operation Peter Pan"[5] program between 1961 and 1963. During this time the United States provided temporary shelters and camps for Cuban children until they were adopted or returned to their parents.

Almost all exiles during the first and second waves settled in the area of southern Florida, particularly Miami, though it was the intention of the United States to relocate them throughout the entire country. Cubans, however, chose Miami based on its proximity to Cuba; for they hoped that they would soon be able to return to their homeland. Additionally, Miami provided a climate and geographical conditions similar to those of Cuba. Many Cubans lived in the community known as Little Havana. The community had the highest concentration of Cubans in the United States and became home to well over 600,000 Cubans.6 At the time of the Cubans' arrival, Miami was a resort town for tourists. It was quickly transformed into a busy city consumed by economic activity and social mayhem swallowed by Cuban culture.

The rent was low enough in Miami for several families to afford one apartment, but it became extremely difficult to find a job. Cubans who were doctors and lawyers in their homeland became maids and dishwashers in the United States, losing all professional status and credibility. They became so desperate for money that they took any job available. Many Cubans, especially the freedom fighters earned a position on the CIA's payroll as they continued to fight for their anti-Castro ideals.7 Nearby, Americans soon felt resentment towards the overbearing, loud Cubans and refused to offer jobs to Spanish-speaking exiles. The United States government did help to offset the hardships of the Cuban exiles by funding the Cuban Refugee Program.8 This program provided free medical attention and groceries to needy arrivals as they helped them to adjust to a new life in a new land.

In 1962, Castro ended all commercial flights to and from Cuba, which slowed migration down, but did not end it. Exiles would risk their lives as they left their homeland on boats and rafts to travel the grueling 90 miles to freedom. During this exodus, members of the lower class, such as blue-collar workers, farmers, fishers and clerical members fled due to food rationing and forced military service. By 1965, 30,000 Cubans had arrived in the United States. Castro launched a surprise policy on the United States allowing any Cuban with family in the United States to leave Cuba from a port located in Camarioca. Many members franticly sailed from Cuba as 5,000 made the dangerous trip to Florida before the United States halted any further boat trips. In creating this policy, Castro tried to prove to the world that he controlled Cuban migration into America, as opposed to the United States that initially viewed these immigrants as illegal.

In response, to this influx of illegal Cubans into Southern Florida, Lyndon B. Johnson stood under the Statue of Liberty and announced that the government would freely accept Cubans in search of freedom, under the provisions that they arrived in an orderly and legal manner. Within the next month, Johnson's administration negotiated the "Memorandum of Understanding," allowing Cubans with relatives already in the United States to emigrate out of Cuba. This agreement called for "Freedom Flights" from Cuba to America. Johnson soon extended this policy of open arms toward Cubans fleeing communism, and then almost one year after the announcement of the Cuban Adjustment Act, he signed it into law. By 1973, Fidel Castro discontinued the "Freedom Flights" to America though approximately 300,000 Cubans had already entered the United States.

Cubans who came into this country in the first wave never really became assimilated into American society. They opted out of participating in politics claiming not to want to lose their roots by becoming involved. This attitude of Cubans and Cuban-Americans changed in the 1970's when those sons and daughters of first wave Cubans chose to adopt American policies. This younger generation of Cubans actively participated in American politics, registering to vote because of their interest in changing foreign policy. One example of this was the election of Xavier Suarez in the late 1980's, Miami's first Cuban-born mayor.

Within Cuban communities, as political awareness and activism increased, political machines began to develop. These political machines were similar in theory to that of William Tweed. As Cubans shared the same interests and beliefs regarding political ideals, their candidates flourished in the vote tally with increasingly more Cubans registered to vote. This involvement was in part a response to their resentment of President John F. Kennedy for letting them down in the Bay of Pigs fiasco. As a result, many Cubans adopted the Republican Party and provided numerous votes for Republican candidates.

Cubans had extraordinarily high expectations for the quality of education for their children. Cuban parents, especially those in the elite class, insisted that their children attend school and stressed the importance of learning English. The belief that, "You can lose your house, your farm, your business or even your homeland, but a good education is something no one can take away from you,"[9] was held by most Cubans because education was known by many as the only asset that would go with them wherever they went. Many of these children continued on to college to earn professional degrees in a wide range of career fields. Cubans became the most likely to complete high school over any other Hispanic immigrant group. The United States government funded the Cuban Student Loan Program to assist Cubans who wanted to go to college. Upon completing college, many would return to Miami where they found increased job opportunities. A large population of prosperous Cuban-Americans resided in the Miami area provided for many lucrative business prospects for those seeking work. Others moved to areas such as New York, New Jersey, Chicago and California where jobs were available as a result of the efforts of the Cuban Refugee Center (a service provided to help relocate Cubans throughout the United States). In these areas, communities similar to that of Little Havana in Miami were created, further hindering the natural assimilation of Cubans into American society.

Our Founding Fathers wanted immigrants to adopt and defend their new country. When an immigrant group settles into one region like the Cubans in southern Florida or the Mexicans in the Southwest, assimilation is not easily attained. Many Cuban immigrants did not wish to be full participants in American society unlike earlier immigrants who bade farewell to their native lands when they boarded ships for America. The mother country is right next door for the Cubans who have no desire to become citizens or learn English. When Cubans set up exclusive communities such as Little Havana in Miami they made it clear that they wish to remain proud Cubans.

Italian Immigration
by Andrew Allen

America has always been known as a melting pot of cultures and peoples, and this reputation has made it an immigration Mecca. Hundreds of different ethnicities have poured into this country since its founding, some loved and accepted, and some hated and feared. Italian Americans have been both. Although now mainstays of American culture, when the Italians first arrived they were one of the most detested of all the ethnic groups.

The period of Italian immigration began in 1890, when they were forced to flee their poverty-stricken country and make the unpleasant crossing to America, and lasted into the 20th century. Once here they were often believed to be natural born criminals, hated equally for their Catholicism and their arrival in overwhelming numbers. But through all this hardship the seeds were planted for their permanent acceptance into American culture. They worked hard, which was necessary during the height of the Industrial Revolution, devoutly religious, and deeply committed to family life (it didn't hurt that they made great food, either). All of these things eventually placed them as one of the most significant ethnic groups in American culture. Even if the period of 1890-1910 was one of intense suffering for Italian Americans, it was also a period that would cement them permanently in the heart of this country.

The Italians had, up until the late 19th century, represented a very small percentage of the immigration into America[10].

Italy had just been unified in hopes of redeeming itself to its former glory, but the change was geographical, not psychological. Southern Italy, already agricultural and poor, snapped under the weight of sharing its profits with the industrial North. The two regions hated and feared each other, and their economies floundered from suddenly having to work off the same currency.[11] As Southern Italy sank into massive depression and poverty, many Italians desperately looked across the ocean to America. Around 1880, they began pouring out of Italy and into the United States in large numbers, and by the end of the century nearly a million Italians had emigrated[12].

Italians left the horrible conditions of Southern Italy only to run into even worse ones on the voyage. Surprisingly, many of them traveled on French, British, and German ships, since their native country could not supply enough to carry them and the other countries saw a chance for profit.[13] In his book Schemes to Distribute Immigrants, Samuel Gompers claims, "More than 2,000,000 Italians have come to the United States in the last ten years....Here from a single nationality has been the revenue of $70,000,000 to the steamships."[14] Cramped together in steerage compartments with up to 200 other immigrants, they slept in bunks on burlap sacks filled with straw or grass, using thin sheets of jute as their covers and cork life preservers as their pillows.[15]

When they landed in the New World, Italians immediately began displaying their sense of unity and cultural identity through *padroni*. A *padrone* was a seasoned Italian-American who would wait for his comrades at Ellis Island and, for a price, help guide them through the immigration and inspection process. From there the *padroni* helped his countrymen find jobs, housing, food and community. This cushion of support was specific to the Italians, and while it helped them adjust to their new life and homeland, it also made them more cut off from the rest of America because their groups were so tight-knit.

Whether or not it wanted to admit it, America needed Italians. Though despised and mistrusted, they provided an invaluable work force for the growing nation. As the United States swelled from the Industrial Revolution, massive cities and factories sprung up and grew, creating hundreds of jobs that no one else was willing to do. The Italian immigration during the late 19th century and early 20th flowed mainly to these giant industrial centers in the East and Midwest.[16] When the value of Italian labor became clear, many businesses would hire *padroni* to ensure that there was a steady stream of workers flowing in.[17]

Once they had found a place to settle, Italians eagerly took up work in a wide variety of occupations. A census from 1890 gives us an idea of the kind of jobs they took: 34 percent were laborers, 10 percent were railroad workers, 8 percent were miners, 6 percent were merchants, 4 percent were farm laborers, 3 percent were peddlers, barbers, or shoemakers, and 2 percent were tailors or farmers.[18] The women of the families usually found work too, working in garment workrooms, factories, and in homes as cloth finishers.[19] As for the children, many of them worked as peddlers on city streets and shoe shiners, but there were those who had the opportunity to attend American schools. While there, they became the primary infiltration point American culture had into the Italian community; children were taught American customs, history, morals, and behavioral standards. They were even referred to with Americanized versions of their names, such as Jane instead of Giovanni or Joseph instead of Giuseppe.[20]

One of the key elements of Italian survival in America was their strong family base. A journalist named Nora Marks described the "undisguised family affection among them" when she met Italians at a local Hull House.[21] This and the Catholic church helped Italians come together and gain strength from each other to overcome their obstacles.

The economic struggles of the Italian-Americans were matched, if not exceeded, by their difficulty with other American citizens. Of the many reasons causing this, one of the most obvious was their late arrival in the country. Italy did not fall on times hard enough to drive her citizens out until late in the 19th century, and by the time Italians made it to America the immigrants of past generations felt cemented in their way of life. Italians were intruders. This feeling was only increased by the huge numbers they came in; according to a census of their presence in New York, Italian population jumped from 1,067 in 1860 to 49,514 in 1890. By the turn of the century that population rose to over 100,000.[22] These numbers were daunting to the past generations of American citizens, and they felt threatened by the sudden presence of new faces around them. Angelo Pelligrini, an American Italian writer, described the attitude they were given as "roughly what the attitude of the American has been toward Negroes."[23] John Carr, a writer for *The Outlook* in 1906, verifies this by saying, "They are charged with pauperism, crime, and degraded living, and they are judged unheard and almost unseen. These short and sturdy laborers....deserve better of the country."[24] Italians were also disliked because they were willing to work for such low wages, often effectively stealing many jobs from other struggling immigrant groups. But, perhaps worst of all for the Italians, they were associated with crime. Even before the infamous Mafia, originally a peacekeeping group of vigilantes in their home country, tarnished their reputation, they were considered bad bloods. A *New York Times* editorial from 1897 read, "Those sneaking cowardly Sicilians, the descendants of bandits and assassins, who have transported to this country the lawless passions, the cutthroat practices and the oath bound societies of their native country, are to us pests without mitigation."[25]

These hostile sentiments were, unfortunately, not idle, and they often led to violence. One of the most infamous cases of this occurred in New Orleans on an October night in 1896. Nine Italians had been tried for the murder of a city superintendent and found innocent, and the decision made the citizens so angry they stormed the prison later that day and hanged eleven Italians, two of whom were not even involved in the trial.[26]

Through all of these hardships, the American government remained relatively uninvolved. Any support offered was usually refused, as Italians had pride that would generally not allow them to receive aid. However, it is worth noting that most of the women killed in the infamous Triangle Shirtwaist Fire of 1911 were Italian.[27] This fire was the catalyst that began the Progressive Era, a movement dedicated to improving the working standards for people like Italians. The movement eventually had great success and directly affected the day-to-day life of Italians. Also there to support the Italians was Jane Addams and her Hull House movement. In an article for the *Chicago Tribune*, Nora Marks notes that there were plenty of Italians at the Hull House she visited and that they were relaxed and happy, "The Italians seemed to feel among friends."[28]

Though the Italian-American community suffered hatred and poverty, it built the foundations that would help later generations come into their own amongst their fellow Americans and finally be accepted for the valuable cultural contributions they offered. Their work ethic gained them respect and their strong family ties and religious communities gave them the support structure they needed to push through the hard times and make a life for themselves. Originally, Italians were known as "birds of passage" (immigrants who only intended to stay for a short period, save up money, and then return home). Instead, most of them remained, and their cultural mark is permanent on America.

Throughout the difficulties the Italian Americans faced in the late 19th-early 20th century, they kept striving forward. They had made a difficult journey from poverty just to encounter more of it, but the Industrial Revolution ensured that they were better off than many. They were hated and misunderstood by those around them, but the *padroni*, the church and their strong family ties gave them the power to survive. Their jobs were difficult and they received low wages, but they had the work ethic to make the best of what they were given. The Italian-American experience from 1890-1910 was a vicious one, but it could not keep them down.

German and Polish Immigration
by Greg Kuhn, Keri Fulcher, Helena Peckar

Immigration is the process through which individuals leave their native country to settle in a foreign land. Immigration is what defines the culture of America. In fact, at one point America was merely thirteen colonies of immigrants. As a result of this process, the United States has earned the nickname, "the melting pot." With each coming generation, there are hordes of new immigrants fleeing to America from terror or poverty in their homeland.

Between the 1940s and 1960s, large numbers of German and Polish immigrants came to the United States seeking a better life. They came for many reasons, most importantly to escape the terror that was enveloping all of Europe in the form of World War II. Contrary to their predecessors, these immigrants did not come to America in search of economic relief but rather to avoid persecution. From 1933 to 1945 more than 130,000 Germans crossed the American borders.29 World War II put a stranglehold around Europe and prevented many Europeans from leaving. But with the end of the war in the late 1940s, immigration spiked. During that time, America, along with the rest of the world, feared a communist revolution. Thus, they were cautious and hesitant about receiving the German and Polish immigrants. Although the German and the Polish immigrants greatly aided the U.S. in times of dire need, they were not welcomed by Americans.

The 1940s through the 1960s were some of the most chaotic years in American history. First, President Franklin

D. Roosevelt's New Deal was faltering, and yet he was elected to a historic third term. While World War II was breaking out in Europe, the United States was still trying to maintain its isolationist policy. But this did not stop the U.S. from giving lend-lease aid to the Soviets or the British. At the same time, America was clashing with the Japanese because they would not adopt the United State's Open Door Policy. A series of silent maneuvers led to the U.S. ending all trade with Japan, ultimately causing Japan to attack Pearl Harbor. After the events of December 7, 1941, America mobilized for war and at last brought itself out of the Great Depression. The economy during the war boomed. After the dropping of the atomic bombs, World War II ended and the economy continued upward. The economy was doing so well that it went out of control and inflation skyrocketed. With the war over, the Soviet Union quickly acquired nearly all Eastern European territories and formed communist regimes in each of them. This broke the agreement of the Yalta Conference, and the Cold War began with the commitment of the U.S. to stop the spread of communism. Thanks to the work of Republican Senator Joseph McCarthy, a great fear of subversive communists swept over the entire country. The convictions of Alger Hiss and the Rosenbergs of espionage only added to the fear.

Soon this hype died down and the country entered a new era with Eisenhower's "Dynamic Conservatism." Generally, Eisenhower tried to maintain peace abroad. On the home front, America had reached a time of prosperity. In 1960, sixty percent of Americans owned homes.30 With the baby boom came the rise of the wealthy suburbs. Education and American culture flourished. Then the 1960s erupted with the Civil Rights Movement that also inspired women and other minorities, like Mexicans, to argue for more rights. Young people were beginning to express themselves in a Sexual Revolution, and were devoted to protesting the Vietnam War. Overall, life in America over these two decades was similar to that of a roller coaster, and on that roller coaster came the immigrants.

For example, 1939 was a crucial turning point for the Poles. During that year, the Nazis swept through Poland and executed nearly 18% of the population, totalling almost twelve million people.31 Almost half of those killed were Polish Jews. But in 1945, the Soviet troops drove the Germans out of Poland and although they were immediately hailed as liberators, the tables quickly turned. Stalin, the Marxist Soviet leader, promptly established a communist government in Poland. Under this immature government, all Poles were forbidden to leave the country. This policy lasted until 1956, but many of the Poles who had already escaped still refused to return to their native country. During the 1940s and 1950s, the American government passed a variety of laws to allow these "displaced persons" to come to the United States.32 Many of these refugees united together and formed the Polish American Congress in May 1944. Their main goal as Polish-Americans was to further their advancement in the American society.

Germans had similar reasons for leaving their country. Hitler drove nearly 130,000 Jewish Germans out of Germany and eventually into America, between the years of 1933 and 1945.33 These Germans left because of problems created by Hitler's rise to power, and the affects that World War II had on their lives. Hitler also drove out any non-Jewish German who did not support his regime. These German Americans struggled to adjust to life in the United States. Americans were wary of the new wave of immigrants because of their suspected communist backgrounds.

Life in America was not easy for new Germans and Polish. They struggled with learning the English language and new customs, and many incessantly dealt with intolerant Americans. While they came to America to rid themselves of persecution, that is often what they found. To make the transition process easier on themselves, the majority of Polish and German immigrants stuck together. They formed their own German and Polish neighborhoods and communities. Such communities provided them with a sense of security and familiarity. In these neighborhoods were houses, community centers, churches, schools, and German and Polish shops. During and after World War II, however, most German immigrants, of whom more than eighty percent were Jews, came to America trying to hide their ethnic identity.34 They quickly assimilated into American life and culture. On the other hand, nothing was more important to the Poles than their communities. Each Polish neighborhood was a microcosm of Poland itself. Such districts came to be so important to the immigrants that they risked confrontation and scrutiny to defend them. Even in the 1960s, during the height of the Civil Rights movement, Polish Americans held their ground and blocked any form of attempted integration in their neighborhoods. In the process, they became labeled as racist bigots, hardhats, and rednecks.35 Such actions only compounded Americans' animosity for immigrants.

Although the transition process from their home country to America was difficult, there was not much struggle in finding a job. The immigrants of this era were actually the brightest and most sophisticated the world had ever seen. With World War II raging in the 1940s, there were many jobs to be filled in munitions and similar factories across the country. And even when the war ended, there were still lots of jobs available. Most Americans had been saving their money and were ready to begin spending. Thus, car, radio, and other appliance factories were making more products than before. Also, scores of the Germans were farmers and settled in large numbers in the mid-West, including Ohio, Wisconsin, Minnesota, Illinois, Indiana, and Missouri. Their crops supported the entire country and its military. Those who were not farmers often settled in the mid-West cities of Milwaukee, Cincinnati, and St. Louis.36

The Polish, on the other hand, primarily lived in cities and worked in factories. In an anonymous letter sent to Poland from Brooklyn, New York, one Polish immigrant complained about their struggle: "What people from America write to Poland is all bluster; there is not a word of truth. For in America, Poles work like cattle. Where a dog does not want to sit, there the Pole is made to sit, and the poor wretch works because he wants to eat."37 Though it was easy for the Polish to find jobs, this quote shows that the jobs they found were not only demeaning, but did not pay well. The Polish and German immigrants had plenty of opportunity to find jobs in the industrial and agricultural industries of America.

Educational opportunities were not as prevalent as finding a job. During World War II, general high school enrollment in America declined. This is because many young men left to get a full time job or join the military. A large majority of these working young men were immigrants who had to work in order to support their families. Part of their communities, the German and Polish schools were vital to the education of immigrant children. As time progressed into the 1960s, however, student enrollment in high schools and colleges drastically increased.

From 1940 to 1960, many laws were passed to restrict the number of immigrants entering the United States and to set limits on the rights of recent arrivals. This was the result of the fear of Communism that had gripped the entire nation. Americans had already experienced the wrath of Nazi Germany in World War II and were in the midst of the Cold War with the Soviet Union. Also, Americans were worried that these immigrants would take all the available jobs because they were willing to work for less money. Thus, Loyalty Boards were established to investigate individuals suspected of being disloyal to the country. In the six years between 1947 and 1953 a staggering 26,236 people were examined, 4,000 of whom went to trial. Going another step further, the Subversive Activities Control Board decided which organizations were communist and then disposed of their propaganda. The Smith Act of 1940 made it illegal to be part of an organization that was at all anti-government. A series of other acts, including the Taft-Hartley Act (1947), The Internal Security Act (1950), and the Communist Control Act (1954), further strengthened the power of the federal government while weakening the power of any immigrant or communist. In 1950, a milestone was reached in immigration history. The Immigration and Nationality (McCarran-Walter) Act of 1952 was passed. This act limited immigration from non-white countries and gave the U.S. government the power to deport any subversive persons.38 The paranoia experienced at that time was called the "Red Scare". It was turned into a circus when Joseph McCarthy accused seemingly "all-Americans" of being spies. In general, immigrants of any kind were clearly not welcome in America.

Despite being treated poorly, Polish and German immigrants were a vital asset to the cultural and intellectual progression of the United States. Two of the world's most famous scientists, J. Robert Oppenheimer and Albert Einstein, were both German Jews who came to America in search of a better life. Together, the two men headed the Manhattan Project and brought America into the lead in nuclear technology. Also, Wernher von Braun, another German immigrant, did groundbreaking work with ballistic missiles, which led to the creation of the U.S. space program, NASA. He and his team developed the Jupiter-C, a Redstone Rocket, which launched Explorer 1, the first satellite on the western hemisphere on January 31, 1958. John Louis von Neumann was another famous scientist who immigrated to America. Neumann, a famous Polish mathematician, came to America where he led the way for original research in the creation of the first computer. His IAS Machine became the model for later scientists. He also put his skills in hydrodynamics, ballistics, meteorology, game theory, and statistics to good use during World War II.[39] Without the help of such ingenious immigrants, the results of World War II and the Cold War might not have been as favorable to the United States.

The issue of immigration is an extremely long-lived and constantly debated topic. Each generation of Americans has consistently felt some form of dislike for immigrants. From 1940 through the 1960s, the American people feared the German and Polish immigrants. They feared that the immigrants would steal their jobs and they feared that these European immigrants were communist spies, trying to institute communism in the U.S. Ultimately, the overall fear with every generation is that the immigrants will "un-Americanize" their country, and thus bring it down.

German Immigration
By Lindsey Aitcheson

Distrust! Exploitation! Abuse! Fear! Hatred! These terms all characterize the volatile relationship between native-born Americans and German immigrants in the half-century leading up to and including the First World War. The need for cheap labor during the Industrial Revolution led to the blatant abuse of newcomers to American society. Furthermore, when political turmoil in Europe struck in the early 20th century, Americans reacted with mass hysteria and shunned all references to German culture. In fact, in the thirty years between the beginning of mass-immigration and World War I, no ethnic group faced more prejudice, abuse, and hatred than the German-American population.

In the late 19th century, the floodgates opened as millions of European and Asian immigrants poured into the United States, with thousands arriving at Ellis Island every day. The Germans made up a significant portion of those coming into America with 1,445,181 Germans arriving in the 1880s, and more that 250,000 in 1882 alone.40 While their numbers increased dramatically, German representation in the foreign-born population actually fell from one-half to one-fifth from 1854 through the 1890s as immigrants traveled from dozens of other countries during that same time period.

In the early 19th century, Russian rulers Catherine the Great and Alexander I convinced hundreds of thousands of German farmers to cultivate the Russian steppes. In return, they were to receive exemption from military duty, and the laws against cash grants, religious liberty, and self-rule. Decades later, their descendants became disillusioned with the life they had under such a system and traveled to America in hopes of finding greater opportunities. One hundred twenty thousand of these Germans living in Russia moved to the area between the Mississippi River and the Rocky Mountains [an area known as the "Great American Desert"] between 1872 and 1920.

The German culture developed in the Midwest and remained almost completely isolated from the rest of the nation. Homesteaders formed close-knit ties within their church communities, especially Lutherans and Mennonites. While these immigrants resisted extra-cultural influence, they had a major impact on the rest of the country. They not only utilized old-world farming ideas, but they also brought a variety of grain from Russia known as 'red hard winter wheat', which was significant in allowing the United States to be completely agriculturally self-sufficient. While they played an important role in American farming, Germans, like the Swedes, were perceived as "snotty" because of their detachment from the rest of society. Thus, despite their contributions, they were under-appreciated because of their cultural differences.

Unlike their agriculture-based counterparts, German city-dwellers did not meet with much success. All that seemed to matter to the American economy was quantity, not quality. Skilled laborers such as bakers and furniture workers, who had spent years developing and fine-tuning their skills, were cast off and replaced with those who could get the job done faster. Therefore, high unemployment rates provided a painful sting to the German-American community and those who could find employment were subject to miserable working and living conditions. These laborers were often exploited and forced to work 15- to 18-hour days for very little pay and what money they did receive was barely enough to provide sufficient housing, clothing, and food for themselves and their families. When labor strikes occurred, they were often brought to a halt by police threats and violence.

The rights of German-Americans, as well as all other immigrants, were infringed upon even further as corruption adulterated the democratic process. Politicians prevented immigrants from voting by changing the voting locations and closing them before the workday had ended. They then intimidated those Germans who did arrive and filled the ballot boxes with forged voting slips.

It is no surprise that Germans flocked to labor unions for support. In 1886, one-third of union members in Chicago were of German descent and of all foreign cultures, Germans contributed the most members to these labor unions.41 These unions were not looked upon favorably by all, however; for instance, the Railroad Strike of 1877 caused much hatred of Germans. The real spark of terror though, was the Haymarket Riot. On May 4, 1886, a bomb was thrown at a police officer during a protest. In response, the officer fired randomly into the crowd. While guilt was never proven, eight were tried in the incident and four were hanged, three of whom were Germans.

Despite the injustices done to Germans, a wave of ethnic pride swept through the nation in the 1890s and 1900s. Of the 800 German publications that were in print in 1890, many of them began to focus on the fatherland. Over time, organizations celebrating German culture arose. The most famous of these was the German-American National Alliance in 1907, which was the brainchild of Charles J. Hexamer, an American-born engineer from Philadelphia.

Not all Americans looked upon these organizations favorably. Many became afraid that Germany's Kaiser Wilhelm was trying to build an empire and promote it through such organizations. In response, they created anti-German organizations that, according to German-American Richard Bartholdt, spread anti-German sentiment "like mushrooms, just as if the devil had traveled over the country and sown poisoned seeds everywhere."42 The government was not sympathetic toward the German population, and introduced such groups as the Immigration Restriction League and the American Protective Association. These groups sought to limit immigration, require immigrants to learn English, and establish laws favoring the prohibition of alcoholic beverages, all of which the Germans strongly opposed.

In 1894, President Theodore Roosevelt delivered a speech entitled "What 'Americanism' Means," which blatantly ridiculed all persons of foreign origin who tried to retain their old culture in a new land.

> The immigrant cannot possibly remain what he was, or continue to be a member of the Old-World society. If he tries to retain his old language, in a few generations it becomes a barbarous jargon; if he tries to retain his old customs and ways of life, in a few generations he becomes an uncouth boor. He has cut himself off from the Old World, and cannot retain his connection with it; and if he wishes ever to amount to anything he must throw himself heart and soul, and without reservation, into the new life to which he has come.43

In this speech, President Roosevelt coined the term "hyphenate" [as in German-American or Irish-American, as opposed to American]. This term entered the popular vernacular and was then used to insult anyone who felt strongly about his national identity.

Relations between German-Americans and Nativists continued to regress as a series of events unfolded. In early 1915, just after World War I broke out in Europe, Americans began to hear about German atrocities in Belgium and increased signs of hostility. In 1915, President Woodrow Wilson delivered a State of the Union address that was directed at German immigrants.

> "I am sorry to say that the gravest threats against our national peace and safety have been uttered within our own borders. There are citizens of the United States, I blush to admit, born under other flags but welcomed under our generous naturalization laws to the full freedom and opportunity of America, who have poured the poison of disloyalty into the very arteries of our national life; who have sought to bring the authority and good name of our Government into contempt." 44

Then in May of that same year the *Lusitania*, sister ship to the infamous *Titanic*, was sunk by German untersee boats [also known as U-Boats]. Over 1,200 people were killed aboard the British ship, including 124 American citizens.[6][45] While German immigrants sympathized with the United States, they also made excuses for the actions of the Germans. Germany warned the United States not to put passengers on

British ships and Americans responded with outright hatred and intense suspicion.

On January 19, 1917, U.S. Intelligence intercepted the Zimmerman Telegram. This telegram, sent by German Secretary of State to the German Minister to Mexico, stated that, in return for support against the American military, Germany "shall give general financial support, and it is understood that Mexico is to reconquer the lost territory in New Mexico, Texas, and Arizona."46 Upon hearing of the proposed agreement, Americans became outraged and launched into extreme anti-German hysteria.

The United States government immediately declared war on Germany and from that point on, German immigrants suffered. They were intimidated into buying Liberty Bonds, which supported the war against their native country. They were imprisoned for making disloyal remarks, forced to kiss the American flag, flogged, and sometimes even tarred and feathered. Anything relating to Germany came under severe scrutiny; the playing of Beethoven was banned in Pittsburgh; Dr. Karl Muck, the German-born conductor of the Boston Symphony, was arrested for "being a threat to public safety;" statues of Johann Goethe and Friedrich Schiller were removed from public places. In schools, German language classes were dropped from the curriculum and German textbooks were banned. In 1917, a new law mandated that German newspapers be submitted in English to the Postmaster for review. According to Theodore Ladenburger, a German-American from New York City, "from the moment that the United States had declared war on Germany," he was made to feel like "a traitor to his adopted country."

"Those war years were really pathetic. You couldn't walk the street with a German paper under your arm. You'd be abused from one end of the block to the other. They went so far they abused the poor little German dogs that walked the streets. That's the hatred that was."47

The hysteria became quite unreasonable when entire towns were renamed in order to try and eliminate the German influence in the country. Germantown, Nebraska was renamed Garland. Berlin, Iowa became the city of Lincoln. Even foods and diseases were renamed; hamburgers soon became known as Liberty steak, sauerkraut as Liberty cabbage, and the German measles as the Liberty measles.

On April 4, 1918, a group of coal miners from Maryville Illinois surrounded a fellow co-worker named Paul Prager, a German immigrant whom they suspected to be a spy. In a humiliating ceremony, they forced him to "prove" his patriotism by kissing an American flag and singing patriotic songs. They questioned him in front of the gathering crowd about his ties to the German government, and then proceeded to lynch him.

It was events like these that instilled fear of society in the German immigrants. When the German-American Alliance came crashing down in 1918, German cultural association membership across the nation plummeted. Immigrants stopped speaking German, even in the privacy of their own homes, and even forbade their children from speaking in their native tongue. Germans rushed by the thousands to try and become American citizens, and hundreds of Germans changed their names to sound more "American." Some church groups continued celebrating German heritage, but failed in the long run as German-Americans as a whole adopted a sense of "cultural amnesia."

Life for Germans in America between the Industrial Revolution and the First World War was rough. As world conflicts and American fears escalated, the mistreatment of Germans was also growing. They were exploited by the American job market; they suffered name-calling, harassment, humiliation, violence, wrongful imprisonment, and sometimes even death solely because of their country of origin. It was not until President Kennedy's "Ich Bin Ein Berliner" speech nearly half-century after World War I, that America tried to restore any dignity to the German culture.

Hungarian Immigration
by Asmir Loncarevic

The United States of America is a nation composed of immigrants from all over the world. The fact that so many nationalities and cultures co-exist in such an ethnically diverse nation is the trait that makes America so inviting for others. In turn, America is a great, established country. The Hungarian, while not the majority of immigrants who came to the United States, arrived post-World War II. They have enabled America, as a "nation of immigrants", to grow culturally. The immigration policies of the 1940s and the 1950s allowed such groups as the Hungarians to immigrate to the United States. But the Hungarian immigrants' arrival to the United States received a welcome unlike any other. The cultural differences that came with them represent the idea that the United States will remain a nation of immigrants for years to come.

As World War II ended, the American immigration policy remained the same. Anti-Semitic or anti-immigrant, many Americans expressed sympathy for victims of the war but believed that the victims should start new lives in places other than America. In 1946, President Harry Truman issued a directive that allowed 40,000 refugees to immigrate to America.[48] As the Soviet Union became an enemy, the refugee policy of the United States changed dramatically; American policymakers were concerned about rescuing refugees from communism and therefore "financially supported, both openly and covertly, virtually any political entity which proclaimed itself anti-Communist."[49] With that, Congress passed the Displaced Persons Act of 1948, which allowed the United States to admit 400,000 displaced persons between 1948 and 1952.[50] In 1952, Congress passed the McCarran-Walter Act that seemed to keep the 1924 national quotas intact.[51] But, the new law also allowed the government to continue using a provision of the Displaced Persons Act of 1948 called "quota mortgaging," meaning that refugees from communism could use future years' quotas to immigrate to the United States. Another provision of the McCarran-Walter Act was "parole"— allowing the attorney general to temporarily except an unlimited amount of immigrants into the country only for emergencies or reasons "deemed strictly in the public interest." Yet another feature of the McCarran-Walter Act was family reunification, which gave special preference to people wishing to migrate to the United States if they already had relatives living in America, thus enabling many earlier immigrants to bring their close relatives to the United States. As the Displaced Persons (DP) acts expired, Congress passed the Refugee Relief Act of 1953, which authorized 205, 000 people to come to the United States over a two-and-a-half-year period.[52] It is clear that under such acts, the United States government was making an impact on immigration when it allowed over 450,000 refugees to come into America between 1946 and 1954. Of that 450,000 more than 26,000 were Hungarians.[53]

Hungarian immigrants came to America in two separate groups immediately following World War II. About 16, 000 Hungarian DPs entered the United States from 1945 to 1946. The second group, consisting of a little more than 10,000 Hungarian, came between 1947 and 1956. Generally these refugees, from the urban areas of Hungary, were educated.

Bureaucrats, army officers, lawyers, managers, nationalists, and anti-Communists comprised the first group. The second group consisted of political leaders who had tried to work with the Communists (who eventually took over the government). All in all, the two groups did not share the same political views. The political opinions and backgrounds of the second group were considerably different from those who had come thirty to forty years earlier, searching for economic betterment and opportunities. They both agreed that they wanted an independent Hungarian homeland, but they disagreed on the type of government to be established. The earlier group wanted to reestablish a monarchy in Hungary, while the later group was more interested in a democratic or republican form of government.[54]

Furthermore, the newcomers were disadvantaged from the start. In order to immigrate, they had to obtain a "Home and Job Assurance"—a written guarantee, on the part of a U.S. citizen, that the immigrant would have a place to stay and employment in the United States. Since the majority of DPs had no relatives or friends among the Hungarian "old-timers," obtaining these assurances happened largely by chance. With that, church groups and other organizations lent assistance in the resettlement of these new immigrants. Settling in established Hungarian communities in places such as Cleveland and New York City, both groups had few ties with earlier Hungarian immigrants in America and did not mix much with one another. The post-war immigrants obtained work as factory hands, janitors, and manual laborers until they could learn English. The adjustment proved to be exceedingly difficult for the older immigrants who were former journalists, educators, lawyers, military officers, and elected officials.[55]

However, the post-war Hungarian immigrants formed hundreds of organizations to promote Hungarian independence and Hungarian heritage and were very successful at it. Two of these groups were the Fraternal Association of Hungarian Veterans and the Hungarian Movement for Freedom, worldwide organizations that together recruited as many as 100,000 members during the 1950s.[56] But by far, the most successful organization to be transplanted and reorganized in the United States was the Hungarian Scouts' Association. The post-war Hungarian immigrants also founded university extension programs and lecture series. They instilled a strong sense of cultural identity in their offspring through Saturday language school and summer school programs. They rendered new life to the gradually diminishing Hungarian communities by forming new organizations and reviving old ones. The Hungarian immigrants also formed many anti-Communist organizations such as the Hungarian National Committee (HNC), which included a large number of former Hungarian political leaders. Although these organizations started out as nationalist groups, most of them soon became cultural, educational, and social groups, providing a place where postwar Hungarian Americans could meet to socialize and discuss common problems.

In October 1956, the Hungarian people revolted against their Soviet oppressors, tried to overthrow the Communist government and install a new government that promised free elections and other democratic reforms. The new government lasted only a few days before Soviet tanks rolled into Budapest, the capital of Hungary, and crushed the uprising. This created a new wave of Hungarian refugees expected to come to the United States. As the world watched, thousands of brave Hungarian "freedom fighters" battled the tanks with guns and homemade bombs. In the end, 25,000 Hungarians were killed in the fighting. Most of the 200,000 refugees fleeing from the Soviets settled in western European countries, but approximately 41,000 came to the United States[57] and were "admitted ... under the emergency Hungarian Parole Program."[58]

Many Hungarians had expected the United States to step in and help them fight the Soviets. They were disappointed when America did nothing; the United States and Soviet Union were at the beginning of the Cold War and such an action might have led to nuclear war. However, the courage of the freedom fighters aroused the sympathy of the American public. President Dwight Eisenhower used the parole provision of the McCarran-Walter Act to let Hungarians into the United States (Hungarian Parole Program).

The 41,000 refugees who came to America received a warm welcome. An old army post in New Jersey, Camp Kilmer, was reopened and used to house the refugees. Most of the Hungarians who came in 1956 were young, single men and women; two-thirds of them were male, many were students, and very few of them were actual freedom fighters.[59] The refugees of 1956 were different from previous waves in many ways and thus received far better treatment than the previous Hungarian groups. They were welcomed as heroes and received an "outpouring of public support and generosity and a very remarkable resettlement program."[60] They evoked great public sympathy in the United States because of their fight against Communism and numerous opportunities, such as scholarship programs, job placement, and financial assistance were made available to them.[61] Many of them were well-trained technical workers educated by the Communist government and had several years of study under their belt. But the Revolution was unexpected and some 6,000 Displaced Persons were already absorbed by the United States. The Hungarians in Cleveland reacted quickly and determinedly, helping the "56ers" (as they came to be called) blend into American life almost immediately. Moreover, within the first days of the crisis, mass rallies were organized and community organizations initiated relief programs. Volunteer groups and government agencies helped them find homes and jobs. College students held silent marches through downtown Cleveland to demonstrate their solidarity with the Hungarian students killed during the Revolution. Hundreds of young men (most were Hungarian volunteers who already served in the armed forces) volunteered to fight for Hungary. Numerous Hungarian women, old-timers, and "DPs" alike, lent their assistance during the crisis by collecting relief funds for the refugees.[62] They made and distributed paper flowers as a small token of gratitude to all who donated. Several relief programs were established by the community, following the tragic end of the Revolution—the largest of these was the Hungarian Freedom Fund, formed under the auspices of the United Hungarian Societies.[63] Through the fund, citizens of Greater Cleveland contributed $47,796 in humanitarian cargo that was then sent to Hungary. A donated amount of $67, 000 enabled the resettlement of 6,511 Hungarian refugees in the Cleveland area.[64] The fund provided financial aid, housing, furnishings, clothing in addition to securing employment and covering medical bills. Included in the figure of 6,511 were fifty-four American citizens, born in Cleveland of refugee parents. Other relief efforts organized by the Cleveland community included the Hungarian Central Committee for Books and Education, which was established to provide educational programs for children in western Europe whose parents had been killed by the Revolution. In addition to sending Hungarian books to the schools housing the orphans, the committee campaigned for their financial support and for the publication of educational materials.[65] But problems developed when refugees in different areas of the United States drifted to Cleveland after losing their first jobs. Despite the fact that the newcomers adjusted with greater ease than previous waves, due to their youth and the opportunities they were offered, problems arose due to the sudden and drastic changes in their lives. However, with the American economy booming, the nation needed more skilled workers. The Hungarians' training and skills enabled them to get good jobs. Many of them soon married Americans from other ethnic groups, with the hopes to stay and become American citizens.

It is difficult to determine the exact number of Hungarian refugees who settled in Cleveland after 1956. United States Census data of 1950 and 1960 demonstrate a significant increase in the Hungarian foreign-born population of Cleveland: more than 4,000 Hungarians of foreign birth settled in the Buckeye Road neighborhood.[66] Other cities bordering Cleveland such as Lakewood, Euclid, Cleveland Heights, and Shaker Heights were each augmented by approximately 1,000 while the city Parma increased by over 2,000.[67]

For several years, many of the "56ers" had little to do with the established Hungarian-American community. But in the 1970s and 1980s, they began to search out Hungarian-American organizations. They had a new desire to share their native language and cultural heritage with their American-born children. By the late 1940s, the sons and daughters of earlier Hungarian immigrants were already moving up into the middle class and out to the suburbs. As is true of virtually every other immigrant group, second- and third-generation Hungarian-Americans were far more American than Hungarian. Their primary language was English and many had little interest in the culture and customs of their parents' native land. The "DPs" and the refugees of the 1956 revolution helped revitalize the Hungarian-American community. Their new clubs and organizations, as well as the Hungarian-American press, became centers for preserving Hungarian language and culture. With the 1960s came a general revival of ethnic life, not only in the Hungarian-American community, but in others as well. People began once again to take an interest in their heritage and make efforts to understand and preserve it.

As can be seen, the Hungarians' warm reception in the United States was unlike any other. Furthermore, it had an influence on setting the precedent for refugees seeking asylum. First, the fighting, then fleeing from the imposing Soviet Union "made them worthy adornments to American democracy."[68] The United States, as Rhatican puts it, "is a draw for millions of immigrants and for specific refugee groups has not only extended asylum, it has positively welcomed them, particularly if they are victims of the United States' ideological adversary."[69] In receiving the "refugees of 1956" and the groups of Hungarian immigrants that came before them, the United States enabled itself to grow more culturally in the same process as establishing itself further as a "nation of immigrants".

The Emerald Tides
Irish Immigration in the 1850s
Michael Einbinder

When the Potato Famine hit Ireland like a ton of worthless soil, many began to turn to the New World to support them now that the Old one had run dry. Shipping themselves across the Atlantic in aging passenger transports, most began new lives in the Mid-Atlantic area, especially New York, Massachusetts, and New Jersey. Upon arrival, they found a less-than-overwhelming welcome, because their influx continued a cycle of the intolerance of large groups of immigrants.

Overpopulated and with high unemployment, the Irish in their native land still stubbornly clung to the soil, even though it gained them nothing. According to an 1835 survey, more than two million people were without regular employment of any sort.70 In 1841, when it became abundantly clear that the population was growing (and growing, and growing) without any sign of slowing down, it was commented that Ireland was probably the most densely populated country in Europe.71

Why the Irish stuck to their patches of land is anybody's guess, but the probable cause is rooted in tradition and the seemingly cultural intransigence inherited by anyone with a drop of Irish blood in them. The soil had served them well for hundreds of years, even though the arable land was three-fourths taken by "cash crops" such as corn, wheat, and barley, which was immediately shipped to England for sale at cheap prices. The remaining land was given to the millions of Irish to do with as they saw fit, and there was only one crop that they farmed in abundance: the potato. It was cheap, easy to cultivate, nutritious, and the scraps were good for the farm animals as well. In short, the potato was the ideal crop for a tightly packed, cash-strapped society like that of the Irish.

When the blight (a windborne fungus) struck the potato crop, and rendered it useless, the Irish tried to turn to their government in Great Britain for aid, with little result. Their pleas were generally snubbed by the English, who considered the Irish second-class citizens (and that just barely), claiming that they were already taxed less heavily than the average British citizen (never mind that the average British citizen usually was better able to meet the tax demands placed upon them by Parliament). In fact, the <u>London Times</u> went so far as to print a scathing editorial on the Irish supplications for aid, stating that "she (Ireland) has contributed to the public revenue not more than one-sixth of the whole – from several of the more oppressive taxes she has been entirely absolved – she has devolved on England a debt contracted before the union, the interest of which equals or nearly equals all that she now remits to the Imperial Treasury, she costs annually half of what she yields in the way of taxation..."72

With no help forthcoming from their own government, the Irish began to look west, and began setting sail into the setting sun in hopes of finding the dawn of a new life. For the most part, they did find new lives in America, not as farmers, but as manual laborers. Crammed into the tenement housing of New England that all émigrés seemed to pass through at one point during those times, they were greeted with a certain amount of reserve on the part of the indigenous population; Protestants of the Northeast came close to suffering a collective apoplexy at the sight of a huddled mass of Catholics at the Golden Door. In fact, between 1845 and 1855, some 1.8 million Irishmen, -women, and -children made the journey to America73, only to find that they had little money to support themselves when they arrived.

Upon arriving virtually penniless in the "Land of Opportunity," they were immediately snapped up by work gangs on the lookout for strong workers willing to labor for low wages doing dirty, dangerous work. In fact, with Irishmen wandering hither and thither in search of wages that would support him and his (often) large family, it was said that for the "poor Irishman, the wheelbarrow is his country."74 While some did manage to climb the social ladder, becoming foremen and overseers in some industrial positions, most were doomed to follow the lot of a servant to a richer family. This brought them into conflict with free blacks (also very poor), fomenting animosity between the Irish, blacks, and abolitionists. In addition to the competition with blacks for unskilled labor, Irishmen managed to snag enough skilled and semiskilled jobs to cause clashes with native-born white workers.75

The workplace wasn't the only area the Irish often found themselves victims of prejudice. Being overwhelmingly Catholic, the Irish immigrants were disliked immediately by the mostly Protestant North Americans. In response to the expanding number of Catholics settling in the country, the Protestants began to lash out politically, bringing about the rise of so-called "nativist" groups. Starting out as local activist groups, many took root in local, state, and even national politics (in fact one, the Order of the Star-Spangled Banner eventually metamorphosed into the "Know-Nothing Party;" a strong political force in the 1850s76).

Because of its comparative compassion for recent immigrants, and also in response to the right-winged nativists, many Irish became fiercely Democratic. The Whig party was the champion of abolition (detested because free blacks meant more competition for jobs), temperance ("Irish" had become synonymous with "heavy drinker"), and anti-Catholicism. Public school reform was on the Whig agenda, but given their intolerance of immigrants and Catholics, it was seen as a threat to the culture as a whole, and the Catholicism of Irish children.

In addition to their strong Democratic stances, many Irish were highly active in labor union organization, believing "that they could gain more by unions and strikes than by plowing and planting."77 They became involved in everything from the Knights of Labor on down through the local levels. The decision from *Commonwealth v. Hunt* ruling labor unions legal only fired their ambitions, though most were simply fired out of hand because they did not constitute a large part of the workforce. The desire to stay in the city and become industrial laborers is somewhat, but not altogether, surprising in that they had come from a highly agrarian society, and then completely abandoned the work of their forefathers in favor of the new type of work to be found in post-Industrial Revolution America, and their stubbornness in dealing with other union organizers foreshadowed the typical Irish tenacity when involved in politics. (and any other sort of activity involving argument).

While conflict raged all around them, the Irish, jammed into their cheap, overcrowded apartment slums, became extremely socially oriented. They formed social organizations that involved entire communities, knitting them together in a huge Irish patchwork. As more of their countrymen arrived, they found an expanding base upon which they could get their social, religious, economic, and political footing in a strange New World.78 Unfortunately for the Irish, their clannish attitudes towards outsiders made for friction between the now-entrenched Irish and newer non-Irish immigrants vying for their place on the social ladder.

The treatment of the new arrivals - mostly Mediterranean and Eastern Europeans - by the Irish is typical of the behavioral patterns displayed by successive immigrant groups. That is to say, when a group arrived, it was usually the target of scorn and prejudice. Once the group had established itself in the natural order of things, another ethnic group barged in. The newly Americanized group would feel superior and threatened at the same time by the newbies, and proceed to discriminate against them, just as they had been segregated, spit upon, and pushed around when they first arrived. The Irish managed to dig in and hold on, and eventually work their way into some of the choice jobs in labor and politics, so they were in a better position than most to harass the newcomers while aiding their incoming brothers and sisters.

Irish Immigration
by Michael Rosenthal-Mix

Off the west coast of England, there is a small green isle revered in lore and marred by tragedy and war. That tragic island was the source of the largest single group of immigrants to the United States up to that time. The Irish Famine that turned two million into refugees has forever changed Ireland and the United States. As most large ethnic refugees are labeled by the native born locals, the Irish were demeaned by racial stereotypes and feared by the uninformed. The natives feared that the Irish immigrants would corrupt government, drain resources, steal and cheat. In the beginning it looked to the Irish like they had landed in another version of a home that did not want them. There were the same draconian laws and the same religious intolerance. Despite that, the Irish survived and grew. They learned about us and we them, for all their hardships, the final destination in their journey ended up at 1600 Pennsylvania Avenue in Washington DC.

In the farms of Ireland there were two distinctly different crops. The potato was grown to feed the Irish. Any disruption in its growth or harvest meant widespread starvation. Cattle, grain, and other foodstuffs were produced, but they were meant for the English. When the potato failed, the most heinous thing was that there was enough food moving through Irish ports that all the starving could have been fed and there would still have been enough for export. While the famine continued, the British did little to help the Irish. They did, however, keep track of how many had died. Chronicled one historian, "The census commissioners calculated that...

the loss of at least 2.5 million persons had taken place."79 In the years between 1846 and 1851 some one million Irish died as a result of malnutrition, while another million left Ireland for good as refugees.80

While the starvation was bad, it wasn't the only thing that pushed the Irish to leave. The other motivator was the law imposed by the English dictating the sale and inheritance of land. In a small place like Ireland, land is more important than any amount of money and the Irish were all but locked out of it. Irish Catholics were banned from buying land and if they had any it was nearly impossible to keep. Instead of land passing to the eldest upon the father's death, it was spilt between all his children.81 In just a few short years, even a large farm would become a hodgepodge of small farms. Eventually the land would be a dead weight to its Catholic owner, and on receiving an offer, he would likely sell it to a Protestant. By the time of the famine, absentee British Protestants owned most of the land in Ireland.

The blight that destroyed the potato crop first struck in 1845, but the worst years were not until 1859-60. Virtually over night, the potatoes were ruined. "In one instance the farmer had been digging potatoes-the finest he had ever seen... up to Monday last; on digging in the same field on Tuesday he found the tubers blasted, and unfit for the use of man or beast."82 The pre-famine population of Ireland had been 8.1 million.83 Ten years after the famine, the population had only moved back up to 6.5 million. While many did die, many more left their homes and their country for far off lands such as Australia, Canada and the United States.

The majority of the Irish immigrated to the United States.84 The arrival of all these destitute refugees, whose deeply felt religiousness was at odds with mainstream protestant America, was not the best of introductions in recorded history. The Irish were met with bigotry and restrictive laws much like the ones they had emigrated to leave behind. In the United States, the Irish found a country less than thrilled to see them. Their huge numbers were a little off putting to local Protestants, former Irishman included. Though the Irish had escaped a land where they were treated as expendable scum, the new country was not too much better.

The most vocal objections to Irish immigration came from the Know Nothings, a political party formed by nativists whose goal was to restrict immigration. The Know Nothings won by landslides in the 1850's throughout the Northeast where most immigrants were settling. During the 1854 election in Massachusetts, in every electable office Know Nothings were the working majority. In the state congress, out of 378 state representatives, 376 were Know Nothings. This super majority allowed for some true pieces of work to be passed. One revealing example was a law preventing immigrants from voting until they had been confirmed residences of the state for 21 years. This law even applied to naturalized citizens. Another example was a law that precluded immigrants from holding public office.

The Irish who arrived during the famine were an agrarian lot, and as such, they had virtually no skills in an industrial society. On top of that, they were in a completely different environment, like being in another world. In order to cope, they brought with them the basic Irish cultural unit, the Parish.

The Irish were very social and faithful; the Irish Catholic Church reflected that. In Ireland it is still the center of village life and most of the activities are either held there or organized through it. In America, with most Irish immigrants in major cities, the local church took on new meaning. It was one of the few reminders of home that the Irish were proud to keep. The churched served another purpose; "to protect its parishioners against bigots with high walls that no missile could pierce and equally high walls of sympathy and commiseration born from a similar situation."85 This thick skin was also a throwback to the old country where the English had outlawed the practice of Catholicism.

The church was perceived in many lights by the Irish and the local born Americans. Thomas Nast a famous political cartoonist and nativist showed the church as an anti-democratic institution attacking virtuous Protestants at every turn. One of his cartoons has wave after wave of bishop alligators descending on the defenseless Americans with the Vatican looming in the background, with the words "political body" and an Irish harp clearly visible.86 This view of the church as an overtly political body was not unfounded. The first generation Irish had tripled the number of Catholics in America most of which were regular churchgoers. They held great respect for the local priest and who could have a great deal of influence in how his flock would vote.

From the 1830s through the 1860s, one of the most powerful men in New York City was Archbishop "Dagger" John Hughes, leader of all Catholics in the city. In 1844, the mayor elect James Harper had campaigned on a nativist anti-Catholic ticket. Hughes told Harper that if even one church was threatened or burned, he would make New York look like a "second Moscow."87 As anti-Catholic mobs had made Philadelphia a war zone earlier that year, Harper took him seriously. In New York, thanks to Hughes' warning, no churches were harmed and the police actually investigated any threats that were made. Later on, when Harper's friends went to the streets, Hughes summoned 3,000 Irish men to defend his churches. Again, violence was avoided. It was a powerful show of Hughes' power.

This power was mainly derived from the Irish's numbers. Before the famine, there had been around 660, 000 Catholics in the U.S. After the first waves of Irish came, that number had swelled to more than a million. This massive influx was largely confined to eastern cities where the impact was magnified. While the Irish had made the American Catholic Church a real player in the U.S., the original European Catholics who had preceded the Irish were not pleased with the Irish presence in their churches. With the Irish as the dominant ethnic group, the American church became more like traditional Irish churches. Irish ministers expected daily attendance. Italian priests, on the other hand, would not have. The Italians were more likely to attend Sunday mass and skip the weekday sermons. Under a German American Catholic church, the parish featured extensive input from the lay people, a practice unheard of in the unflinchingly hierarchical Irish church. Some disagreements over structure and conduct were so strong that some minority Catholics demanded separate churches that would reflect their values. These splits served to further separate and segregate the already isolated Irish community.

Isolation often leads to paranoia about the world. Once in New York City, Irishmen threatened to disrupt the inauguration of the Brooklyn Bridge because the date happened to be the Queen of England's birthday. Despite having elected its first Irish mayor just two years earlier, some Irish were not convinced.88

The devoutness felt by the Irish helped them to cope when they first arrived and to give them a united political voice later on. As the second generation Irish were growing up in the U.S., their parents had made sure that they would be safe from racism and educated in schools not run by Protestant reformers. These children had access to Catholic services from birth to death. They could be born in a Catholic hospital, educated in Catholic schools like Notre Dame, Loyola and Villanova. They could be married in the church they were baptized in and then buried in that same church after they had died. The American church had enormous influence over its members' ethics, politics, sexual mores and beliefs. This inspired a fairly parochial populace, one that knew very little of the outside world, but that could not stop change for long. At first the cracks in the churches' control were small, an Irish Catholic marrying an Italian; but then the cracks grew bigger. The best Irish American writers wrote scathing books about the small mindedness of their people, of the churches' hypocrisy and spiritual emptiness. As society marched on soon a mixed marriage was a Catholic and a Protestant or a Jew.

With all the challenges and hardships they faced, the success of the Irish has been amazing. Initially they were resented, then the subject of racial slurs. Now they have so fully assimilated that everyone looks forward to St. Patrick's Day each year so everyone can act a little Irish.

The Great Irish Struggle

By Eric Ahle, Chris Cutting, and Phil Smith

To think that any immigrant group that came to the United States had it easy is to tell a lie, especially when you talk about the Irish. They ventured across the Atlantic Ocean in search of economic and civil relief. There is no episode in American history that can either relate to or compare with the hardships that the Irish endured, not only in their homeland of Ireland, but in the United States as well.

Before the Great Famine, Ireland was a land under conquest of England, whose economy relied heavily on the agriculture and farming put forth by impoverished Catholic peasants89. Despite the Irish political subordination, the pre-famine society, though somewhat restricted, was operational and fit for human habitation. This economic stability could be traced back to one thing.

This dense population in Ireland, "deep in poverty, tied to the land by history and custom, overlooked by the Industrial Revolution, relied on only one crop itself – the potato."90 The potato was very easy to grow, even with very poor, infertile land conditions. They could feed many mouths without taking so many laborers, time, or land. An acre and a half of potatoes could feed a family of six. It has been estimated that a third of the Irish poor, much of the population, ate almost nothing else, and it formed the bulk of the diet for many more.

The greatest drawback of the potato was its susceptibility to disease, particularly the fungus *Phytophthora Infestans,* commonly known as the potato blight.91 This fungus, carried by the wind, rain and insects, was brought right onto the land of the Irish. As the potato was such a staple in the Irish diet, and the majority of the population was either growing it or eating it, the fungus was able to spread rapidly throughout the countryside. This would be the prelude to one of the greatest famines in the history of the world, not to mention one of the greatest migrations into the United States.

Little did they know that the crop that had fed them and supported the country's economy would eventually lead to the demise and collapse of the very lives they had known. "Coming on the harvest time of the year 1845, the crops looked splendid, but one fine morning in July, there was a cry around that some blight had struck the potato stalks," remembered an emigrant from west Munster, "the air was laden with a sickly odor of decay, as if the hand of death had stricken the potato field, and everything growing in it was rotten."92

The Irish countryside of the 19th century, especially from 1845 to 1855, was filled with vast amounts of people, as it was "...the most densely populated country in Europe."93 Though one is trained to believe that so many people could only live in an organized environment such as a village or set community, these people were forced to live in horrendous conditions that subjected them to diseases such as typhus and cholera. They also slept alongside cattle, pigs, and other farm animals. Approximately 1.5 million deaths could be attributed to this famine and disease.

The population of Ireland saw a significant fluctuation in numbers prior to the famine due to the Napoleonic Wars, as refugees fled to Ireland from their war-torn homelands. During the years of the famine, however, because of such poor living conditions, disease, and hunger, a large number of Irish men, women, and children migrated all over the world.

From 1831 to 1840, the number of immigrants from Ireland to the United States was approximately 207,000; but during the famine from 1841 to 1850, the number of immigrants entering the United States was significantly raised to 781,000 people.94 Despite the fear, hunger, misery and sickness experienced during the migration, the vision of a new beginning in America kept their hopes alive. Although they now had an opportunity to start a new life in a land they had never seen, but heard only great things about, the daunting task of survival during their voyage was only the beginning of the hardships these immigrants would have to face in order to reach their goal of a new and better life.

> In the foulest stench that can be conceived of, so soon as the eyes had been accustomed to the darkness prevailing everywhere but under the open hatch, a mass of humanity, men, women, and children would be seen lying over each other above the deck, often half naked, many covered with sores and all with filth and vermin to an incredible degree: the greater portion stupefied or in a delirious condition from Typhus or Putrid fever, Cholera and Small Pox: all were helpless and among them were often found bodies of the dead in more or less advanced stages of decomposition.95

Meanwhile, across the Atlantic Ocean in the "Land of Opportunity," the United States was about to begin the Mexican-American War, while President James K. Polk and other politicians were preaching "Manifest Destiny" or the continental expansion of America. Even though the country was expanding west, New York City was one of the many places to be struck hard by the arrival of the Irish and other immigrants in the years to come.

Even before the arrival of the Irish into the gates of any ports in the United States, the "Natives" to the land already had preconceived horrific notions of these strangers. The "Natives" felt that the strangers arriving on their land were uncivilized, drunken fools who should never have come to their nation in the first place. Others saw the opportunity to profit from these people who had nothing to begin with. They had no money, no shelter, and were very vulnerable to acts of debauchery and corruption. Had the immigrants known of the hatred they would face upon entry into this new land, perhaps they would have thought twice about taking the voyage.

"WHY SHOULD I FEAR THE FIRES OF HELL? I've been through Ellis Island," inscribed an immigrant on the wall of the New York City port.96 This is the way all immigrants felt when they entered America through the gates of Ellis Island, as they were ostracized harshly and met by racist comments from the strong Nationalists who believed that these immigrants were degrading the American culture. Bill "The Butcher" Poole, a staunch Nationalist who had an overwhelming hatred of the immigrants, was a prime example of the way many Americans felt towards Irish immigrants.97 Of those Nationalists who did not succeed in keeping the Irish out of "their" country, many would exploit the Irish by tricking the gullible migrants into giving them whatever money or valuables they brought with them to America. Politicians also saw the Irish immigrants as easy votes for their next election, by simply offering "a head start". This "head start" would include such amenities as shelter, work, and pay, all for the low price of a vote, or two or three.

The prejudice and hatred the Irish were subjected to in America led to the establishment of large immigrant based communities, such as the Five Points in New York City. Here, different Irish groups banded together to fight other communities for the right to small pieces of land, or more so, pride and respect. This was all well and good for the Irish to keep themselves occupied, but as far as the corrupt government went, these were merely just votes to keep the "Boss" in office.

> "Think of the hundreds of thousands of foreigners dumped into our city…They are alone, ignorant strangers, a prey to all manner of anarchical and wild notions…And Tammany looks after them for the sake of their votes, grafts them upon the Republic, makes citizens of them in short. . . . If we go down into the gutter it is because there are men in the gutter, and you have to go down where they are if you are to do anything with them."98

Such feelings were very common among the politicians and people in power in New York City at the time. They did not care about the welfare of these people, but rather only for the mere numbers of them at the polls. The illusion of a place to live, which was actually a slum or a barn that had been made into human housing, a community to be a part of, and a land of opportunity was just part of the "Boss'" plan to keep the political machine running at all costs.

Uneducated, unskilled, and unprepared for the American middle class, when it came to the Irish looking for work, they were forced into the lowest part of American society. Work for people like this was limited to manual labor such as working on the New Orleans New Canal and railroads. "Wherever they lived in urban America, in the middle decades of the 19th century, large numbers of Irish were at the very bottom of the economic structure, over-represented as common laborers and domestic servants."99 In 1850, sixty-three percent of the manual laborers in the United States were Irish immigrants, while the native-born only took up about seven percent.

Although a large percentage of the Irish had occupations in manual labor, a small percentage actually fulfilled the "American Dream" they had set out to achieve when making the voyage to the United States. Though many were not schooled or educated in Ireland or America, a few became entrepreneurs.

> "Many who came were not workmen at all, but entrepreneurs. James Phelan is the kind of Irish immigrant not usually discussed. He immigrated to New York and moved on to Cincinnati, where by 1848 he had a wholesale grocery business worth perhaps $40,000. Drawn to San Francisco by the gold rush, he made his first fortune selling provisions to miners and then became a real estate magnate and one of the city's first millionaires. His son, James D. Phelan, became a United States Senator."100

Most of the Irish who came to America still had strong family ties to their loved ones left behind in Ireland. They felt strongly about helping their family accomplish a better life that would bring them away from the poverty stricken societies of Ireland. They sent what little money they could spare so that they could have their family reunited in America, "The Land of Dreams." Letters were written in order to maintain contact with their loved ones:

> "My Dear Father and Mother,
>
> I remit to you in this letter twenty dollars, that is four pounds, thinking it might be some acquisition to you until you might be clearing away from that place altogether, and the sooner the better, for believe me, I could not express how great would be my joy at our seeing you all here together where you would never want to be at a loss for a good breakfast and dinner.
>
> Your ever dear and loving child,
> Margaret McCarthy"101

The cultivation of Irish culture in the United States has been extremely influential to both the Irish and American society. The hardships the Irish endured to be given the name "Irish-American" were so extensive, that hardly anyone will ever understand it the way those who lived through it did. The struggles and battles fought on two fronts, both their homeland, and the New Land, have given them the right to call themselves true Americans. A few people may argue that they do not deserve to be a part of our nation's history; however, just as the Revolutionaries defeated Great Britain, the Irish overcame the overwhelming adversity that was against them.

The Irish: The Riches and the Spoils
by Mallory Abney

Throughout history, people have come to America in search of a new life full of opportunities and without the old problems they left behind in their native countries. Immigrants usually emigrate from their countries because some type of problem or way of life with which they are unable to cope. Although they expected great opportunities in their new environment, they still wanted to retain their old customs and traditions. However, throughout history it has also been known that just as most new immigrant groups are persecuted when they arrive in America, these same immigrants seem to turn around and give the same grief to those who immigrate after them. There are several groups of peoples who immigrated to this country that fit this mold. One of the best examples of this is the Irish that immigrated between the 1840s and the 1850s due to the Potato Famine that struck Ireland.

When the blight (a windborne fungus) struck the potato crop and rendered it useless, the Irish tried to turn to their government in Great Britain for aid. Their pleas were generally snubbed by the English, who considered the Irish second-class citizens, claiming that they were already taxed less heavily than the average British citizen; though the average British citizen was better equipped to meet the tax demands placed upon them by the parliament. In fact, the <u>London Times</u> went so far as to print an editorial on the Irish supplications for aid, stating that "she (Ireland) has contributed to the public revenue not more than one-sixth of the whole – from several of the more oppressive taxes she has been entirely absolved – she has devolved on England a debt contracted before the union, the interest of which equals or nearly equals all that she now remits to the Imperial Treasury, she costs annually half of what she yields in the way of taxation…"102

The Irish, a people with an agriculturally based economy, were subject to the bounty of their crops; therefore when the Potato Famine hit Ireland it was a great loss for many. There were so many Irish families who were affected by the famine, not only their food supply, but because selling their crops was their main source of revenue and income. With no help from their government, the Irish began to look to the west. They began to set sail in hopes of finding a new life. Due to their sudden state of devastation, many Irish families began looking for a way to escape their hardships and thought they had found it in America. Setting sail on poorly made passenger ships, they headed for America, hoping for the best. However, upon arriving on the northeast coast, they ran into an entirely new set of problems. For the most part, they did find new lives in America, not as farmers, but as manual laborers. Crammed into the tenement housings of New England that all émigrés seemed to pass through during those times, they were greeted with a certain amount of indifference on the part of the indigenous population; Protestants of the Northeast came close to suffering a collective apoplexy at the sight of a huddled mass of Catholics at the Golden Door. In fact, between 1845 and 1855, some 1.8 million Irish men, women, and children made the journey to America103, only to find that they had little money to support themselves when they arrived.

Though many families moved to America seeking relief from their troubles in Ireland, many of their fellow countrymen stayed and tried to tough it out. However, due to the overpopulation and lack of work in Ireland, those who stayed behind had a lot of trouble. According to survey taken in 1835, more than two million people were without regular employment of any sort.104 In 1841, when those living in Ireland and in other countries saw that the population was growing exponentially, it was estimated that Ireland was probably the most densely populated country in Europe.105

So, many Irish stayed behind with the land that many of them had had in their families for generations. These people stayed for many years and were determined to make it through the hard time without deserting the land that had treated them well for so many years. Even though the arable land was three-fourths taken by "cash crops" such as corn, wheat, and barley, which was immediately shipped to England for sale at cheap prices, the remaining land was given to the millions of Irish to do with as they saw fit. However, out of all the many "cash crops" they produced, the potato was only one crop that they farmed in abundance. It was easy to cultivate, nutritious, and the scraps were good to give to the farm animals. In short, the potato was the ideal crop for a tightly packed, cash-strapped society like that of the Irish. Not only was it a part of their daily meal, but the potato was so nutritious and useful that it brought in a lot of profit.

With Irishmen wandering in search of wages that would support him and his (often) large family, it was said, "poor Irishman, the wheelbarrow is his country."106 Upon arriving virtually penniless in the "Land of Opportunity," they were immediately grabbed up by gangs on the lookout for strong workers, willing to work for low wages doing the jobs no one else wanted to do. Though some were able to obtain a respectable job and make a living for themselves, many ended up only suffering and slaving in hopes that the future generations of their family would be more successful. Those who obtained respectable jobs still were at the lower end of the economic chain; becoming foremen and overseers in some industrial positions; most were doomed to followers and not leaders for the rest of their lives. This also brought them into conflict with free blacks (also very poor). The growing animosity between the Irish, blacks, and abolitionists made for very hostile situations. Thus, they competed with the Irish and the Irish were immediately persecuted by any poor families or freed slaves who were trying to obtain the same job. In addition to the competition with blacks for unskilled labor, Irishmen managed to snag enough skilled and semiskilled jobs to cause clashes with some native-born white workers.107

The workplace was not the only area the Irish often found themselves victims of prejudice. Being overwhelmingly Catholic, the Irish immigrants were disliked immediately by the mostly Protestant North Americans. In response to the expanding number of Catholics settling in the country, the Protestants began to lash out politically, bringing about the rise of so-called "nativists" groups. Starting out as local activist groups, many took root in local, state, and even national politics (in fact one, the Order of the Star-Spangled Banner eventually metamorphosed into the "Know-Nothing Party;" a strong political force in the 1850s108).

However, even though they were persecuted and treated badly for there first years in the country, they still had prejudiced feelings towards many of the immigrant groups that came to the America after them. Due to this cycle, it is evident that many immigrant groups who come to America, "the land of opportunity", looking for a new life, will be subject to ridicule and persecution, even by other immigrants.

The Irish Arrive
by Audrey Bales

Every immigrant group attempting to assimilate itself into American society meets with disdain and contempt. Of all the many cultures with the achievement of acceptance, the Irish immigrants of the Great Famine experienced the hardest transition. Although leaving one's homeland always proves difficult, as the Irish faced the desolation of their homeland with no help from England, a large number finally immigrated to America and integrated themselves into a culture that abhorred them. They received no help from the government and were shunned by local organizations. The Irish immigrants fought stereotype, war, disease, and poverty of the worst degree. Many grieved at the knowledge that the Emerald Isle, the mythical land of Erin, had been ravaged; millions of people died and millions more lost their homes, families, and futures because of a little fungus called *Phytophthera infestans*.

The Great Famine, also called "An Gorta Mor" or "The Great Hunger" began when every potato harvest from 1845 through the early 1850's failed. Most of Ireland relied heavily upon the production of the potato as their only source of food. Naturally, the annual failures proved devastating. The famine killed over one million Irish and another million fled to America to escape the destruction. The decision to emigrate, however, proved as difficult as trying to survive in Ireland during the Great Hunger.

"The throngs who fled Ireland's Great Hunger
and their children had little choice but to

reinvent who they were. Famine immigrants spilled out of coffin ships into American cities 'dressed in rags, weak with hunger, and numb with the fresh memory of corpse-filled workhouses, skeletal children, and tales of cannibalism,' in Dennis Clark's words. They were pre-modern peasants, 'homeless, nationless, and all but hopeless after a grim sea passage to an unwelcoming land.' "109

Many Irish did not survive the journey across the ocean, dying on the cramped and disease-ridden ships, "coffin ships," before they even saw America. Just in the first portion of the Irish immigration story, the greatest tragedy unfolds: The Irish did not come to America looking for freedom, religious or otherwise; they came because there was no other choice but to escape the disaster and financial crisis of their country.

To make the transition even harder, the present Americans looked down on the Irish immigrants.

"Like the immigrants who would later take their place on the bottom rung of the socioeconomic ladder, they represented much of what upstanding American society abhorred. The Irish were Celts, not Anglo-Saxons; Papists, not Protestants; rebels fighting to expel America's Motherland from their homeland. They were communal in a land of vaunted individualist achievers; drinkers at the dawn of the American temperance movement; a gregarious and boisterous

people who showed little interest in serious
American enterprise but loved politics."110

Anti-Irish and anti-Catholic feelings entered the scene,
causing the immigrants great amounts of strife. The presence
of anti-Irish notices became popular, reading: "No Irish Need
Apply" or "Dogs and Irish Keep Out." Americans stoned
Catholic churches and violence in the streets developed,
such as the Philadelphia Nativist Riots and the New York
City Draft Riots of 1863 during which mobs of mostly Irish
workers rebelled against the unfairness of the draft and its
$300 exemption policy by looting stores and setting fires.

The American government offered no programs and
passed no laws to help the Irish. Some state governments
expressed feelings of deep hostility, such as Boston,
Massachusetts.

> "An historian of the Boston Irish put it this
> way: 'If there had existed in the nineteenth
> century a computer able to digest all the
> appropriate data, it would have reported
> one city in the entire world where an Irish
> Catholic, under any circumstance, should
> never, ever, set foot. That city was Boston,
> Massachusetts. It was an American city with
> an intensely homogeneous Anglo-Saxon
> character, an inbred hostility toward people
> who were Irish, a fierce and violent revulsion
> against all things Roman Catholic...A city that
> rejected the Irish from the very start...'"111

And yet Boston attracted much of the Irish immigrant
population. By 1855, one in every three people living in

Boston was an Irish immigrant. The result was a new political party coming to power: the Know Nothing party. "The Know Nothings were opposed to the immigration of foreigners, especially Irish-Catholics, and believed that 'Americans must rule America,'"112 says Jay Dolan. The party managed to get into office, then passed a series of laws aimed at the Irish Catholic population, including dissolving Irish militia units, dismissing Irish state workers, deporting poor Irish back to Liverpool, and other outrageous laws. In 1856, the party lost public favor and the Know Nothing candidate lost overwhelmingly in the presidential election.

On top of everything else, the conditions in America in the 1840s proved unfavorable for the Irish immigrants. In the political arena, Harrison had just died in office—April 4, 1841—and, "John Tyler was the first vice president to succeed to the office of president on the death of his predecessor."113 Tyler also became the first president to face the possibility of impeachment, due to his virulent opposition to Henry Clay's ideas. Economically, the country was recovering from financial crises in the 1830s. Henry Clay introduced his "American System" program in 1841 which involved the repeal of the independent treasury, the creation of the Third Bank of the United States, the distribution of profits from land sales, the raising of tariffs, and the allowance of squatters to occupy or buy public land, also known as the Preemption Act.114 Basically, America became extremely involved in her own economic and political crises to care too much about the immigrants moving into the States. The Irish Catholics fought their own wars and built their success with their own hands.

Most male and female Irish immigrants worked and either saved the money for themselves and their families, or sent the money back to family in Ireland. Men worked on the Erie Canal, digging and lifting for good wages because no one else would do it. However, the work was dangerous and the sites were disease-infested. They also worked in the mines up and down the East Coast. Immigrant women worked in factories as seamstresses, in hospitals as nurses, or in middle and upper-class homes as domestic servants. By 1855, more than seventy-five percent of New York's 24,000 domestic servants were foreign-born Irish. At the end of the day, the workers went home to dangerous urban ghettos, tenements, or slums. The poverty-stricken Irish crammed 1.82 families into one or two-room residences. Many attempted to survive the bitter winters in pathetic shanties with five to a hut.

> "Bishop John Hughes of New York was in part correct when he admitted that Irish 'abodes in the cellars and garrets' of that city were "not more deplorable nor more squalid than the Irish hovels from which many have been exterminated.' However, inadequate sanitation had potentially more lethal consequences in densely crowded, working-class wards such as the 'Bloody Old Sixth' than in the rural hamlets of his native Tyrone. Furthermore, as Hughes and his fellow churchmen well knew, the conditions of Irish-American working-class life bred or exacerbated severe social problems such as drunkenness, crime, violence, and insanity which both reflected and reinforced economic deprivation and uncertainty.115

Finally, schooling became a huge issue. The same John Hughes created controversy by calling all public schools in America anti-Catholic. In order to appease him, many public school systems grudgingly toned down the religious element in the classrooms. But Hughes was looking for schools that did not merely educate, but also strengthened ties between Irish Catholics. However, the controversy escalated to violence with the Philadelphia Nativist Riots of 1844. The rioting involved property destruction, a few fatalities, and several injuries. So the Irish immigrants created Catholic private schools, ranging from parish grade schools to universities (for example, Loyola University, Boston College, and Notre Dame). These schools served to stabilize the poor Irish immigrants, their children, and their communities.

Through all of this, the Irish thrived and succeeded in assimilating their culture into America. Sadly, it was at a great price. The construction of their school systems, the building of their fortunes, and their war on stereotype only increased the pain of the Irish immigrants forced to evacuate from Ireland. The extreme difficulties they rallied against allowed them the respect they deserved for being the culture of most-burdened immigrants.

Italian Immigrants 1890-1910
by Juliette Fitzsimmons and Emily Hueber

From Southern and Eastern Europe came the "new" wave of immigrants, just after the American Civil War. At this time, the largest group was the Italians who totaled over five million, the majority of them coming from southern Italy, especially Sicily.[116] The reason for their plight was due to high unemployment rates, overpopulation, famine, and deprived agricultural lands in Italy.[117] Additionally, the farmers suffered from falling prices for their produce and Italy was one of the most overpopulated countries in Europe around the late 1800's. However, it is believed that as soon as word spread that America offered high wages and employment opportunities, the word "America" took on an idolized connotation.[118] The majority of the immigrants came from backgrounds with very little education, living in rural communities. Despite this, all newcomers, whether they were Italians, Jews, or Japanese, contributed to the economic expansion of the American society. They were responsible for making America the diverse nation that it is today, while assisting the development of its culture. The rush of Italian immigration to the United States from 1890 to 1910 reflected devastation in Italy and hope in the United States.

The loss of opportunities and the hopes for an escape from poverty stricken Italy drove Italians from both the North and South to the U.S. in search for the "American Dream." The majority of the original immigrants who started coming in 1890, were middle-aged males; Italy lost anywhere from 250,000 to 500,000 citizens a year. However, families of women and children of all ages began to migrate to the U.S. by 1900. Originally, the Italians just wanted to leave the country for a period of time, make their "fortunes" and return with the money. Yet, many Italians realized that settlement in the U.S. was the best opportunity. Most of the Italians could originally only find unskilled work in the major cities of New York, Philadelphia, Chicago, Baltimore, and Detroit. The immigrants were able to develop Italian neighborhoods, which welcomed new immigrants once they reached America. The Italians' dedication to long work and acceptance of low wages made it easy for them to gain industrial work. The Italians dominated construction and provided New York with 75 percent of its bricklayers, builders, and masons. However, the conditions in which they worked were dangerous and any injuries or deaths that resulted were not met with any financial compensation. Despite their farming backgrounds in Italy, most of the Italian residents in the U.S. avoided work in agriculture. The government did not have a large say on the Italian's sudden immigration, because they did not see them as a threat. Rather, they were extra citizens to fill labor work and they were easy to recruit for work at the outbreak of the First World War. However, only one of the dilemmas that the Italians faced was low wages. Although the living conditions for new Italian immigrants in the U.S. were rather harsh, word still traveled back to Italy that it was a much more prosperous environment than their devastated homeland.

At the time of the Italians arrival, mainly between 1890 and 1910, the United States was undergoing some changes of its own as a nation. It was a time between the Civil War and the First World War and the Great Depression. Reformations within the government's structure and goals were occurring.

Migration west was becoming more popular and major cities were industrializing. The industrialization of major cities set the tone for a new economy and a production system that could be beneficial to importing and exporting goods. The industrial ideal required extensive labor and since the economy was low, immigrants who wished for any wages at all were hired instantly. The economy was on an incline because major cities were creating businesses that supported the nation financially. Plus, the growth of cities took away from agriculture and farming, causing those people to move from rural to urban settings. Therefore, America socially was migrating to large cities where opportunities were available to make large amounts of money. So, a hierarchical division of wealth began to develop and a separation between the rich and poor grew to greater disparity. Overall, the economic, political, and social conditions of the United States between 1890 and 1910 welcomed the Italians for the sole purpose of extra hands to work.

The government did not make any special arrangements for the arrival of Italian immigrants. They did not feel it necessary to create special programs because they felt their land was enough of a privilege for them to live on. Plus, the government could not count on the Italians to stay very long and, therefore, had doubts about what to grant them. They did, however, have expectations, most important being the fact that Italians should obtain or practice complete citizenship.[119] This meant that they would learn English, abide by the laws, and contribute to society. Since the government did not recognize the Italians as special, the American citizens did not treat them that way. They were accepted as poor, uneducated, and ungrateful; only were they useful in occupational settings.[120]

In cities like New York and Chicago, where many of the Italians settled, housing was less than satisfactory. Many of the buildings were six or seven stories high with four apartments on each floor. The buildings were built very close together in order to conserve space, yet this only created more problems. All front rooms of the apartments faced the street, in order to receive direct sunlight and fresh air, yet the remaining three or four rooms overlooked airshafts, which let in more soot than oxygen. The lack of clean air in the majority of each apartment led to poor sanitation facilities. All toilets were shared, most of the time overflowing, and the garbage collection was never consistent. Piles collected in the streets for weeks on end, which children played next to daily, and this, along with horse droppings and rats, only added to the unsanitary conditions.[121] Ironically, such conditions would never have been accepted by any Americans but since the Italians had suffered and lived under such awful circumstances in Italy, they were appreciative of any work and any shelter.

In addition to this, the majority of the Italian families could not afford three or four room apartments, thus they brought in lodgers, most of the time relatives, to help create financial stability. This led to overcrowding and to unsanitary conditions already established, which escalated the problems. Epidemics such as the mumps, measles, whooping cough, and scarlet fever spread rapidly and took over many families at a time, mostly the younger members.[122] However, issues such as these could not be addressed because of their low incomes. Regular housing bills could not be paid, let alone medical bills or healthy diets. The financial strains on the Italian immigrants in the U.S. made it difficult for men to support their families, especially if they were still living in Italy.

Italians tried to preserve their culture within their communities, especially as the number of immigrants increased, particularly in the larger cities. Italian-American newspapers were published in major cities starting in the late 1800s. Italian societies maintained their traditions through food, dance, and music, all of which assisted in making the adjustment to America easier. Most Italian children did attend English schools instead of staying within their communities.[123] Additionally, Italian social organizations were set up to help new immigrants find employment, housing, and goods. Their commitment to the Catholic faith drove them to search for churches, but their search only led to Irish churches that lacked their language and culture. Therefore, they built their own churches in which customs of Italian Catholicism could be preserved. Italian immigrants had close family ties to their extended families. Children were raised to be well disciplined and admire the father as the head of the household and the mother as a warm and affectionate figure.[124] The Italians' definition of loyalty was found in their family traditions, which set the tone as an Italian-American supreme obligation. Despite their advancements in adapting to American life, the Italians married within their nationality and maintained a strong cultural unity especially in language, which prevented most of them from fully speaking English.

Americans were quite disrupted by the rush of immigrants from Europe in the 1800s and early 1900s. Italians were criticized and ostracized for their culture throughout their movement in the U.S. Americans were dissatisfied with the Italians' attempt to learn the language or accept the culture of America, though some Italians were only temporary and stayed no longer than five years. Americans felt "used" that Italians were taking advantage of the land that afforded them so many opportunities. Americans felt the Italians showed no appreciation to the country or the American people, which to the American people reflected a lack of loyalty and respect. However, the Italians' main struggles came with the Irish rather than the Americans. The Irish were threatened by Italians taking their work and money, so hostility continued in their disagreeing views on Catholicism and fascism.[125]

It is difficult to define a challenge, when the struggles of Italian immigrants between 1890 and 1910 can surpass any imaginable suffering. Trying to escape the devastating economy, government, and society perpetuated further troubles. They reached America where work was easy, but their quality of life was still substandard. A changing America accepted the immigrants for work and the government accepted them solely as bodies. The Italians were able to reside in communities that exercised their culture, religion, and language to the fullest extent. Yet, their lifestyle made it difficult to define the Italian-American citizens as Italians or Americans. They were born in Italy and most often had grown up there, but they lived and worked in America while practicing the life they would have led back home. The Italians argued that America promised personal rights, and yet the government believed that the Italians should obey their wishes if they were allowing them to reside on their ground. The rush of immigrants from Italy between 1890 and 1910 did indeed reflect devastation back home, and yet the promised hope of America seemed only an illusion to the Italian immigrant. In one man's recollection about his fight for a national identity, he stated, "In Italy they call me an American, but in America, they know immediately that I am Italian."[126]

Italian Immigration 1890-1910
By Eric Davis

Ever since the United States was founded, immigrants have been arriving on its soil. The first white inhabitants of the U.S. were immigrants from Europe. They came for many reasons, such as religion and opportunity. As the country grew and became more prosperous, it became more enticing to foreigners looking for opportunity. This continued into the 20th century and finally during the early 1900s, the United States began to restrict immigrants from coming to their country, mostly for cultural and economic reasons. Even the immigrants who were allowed in during the 1920s faced many hardships such as religious persecution, racism, and xenophobia. One of the major groups of immigrants during that time was the Italians. Many wonder if the Italian immigrants' experiences showed the overall immigrant experience during the 1900s. The Italians provide us with a wonderful look into the common immigrant experience due to their large numbers and their wide range of settlement throughout the United States.

During the period from 1900 to 1910, 4,652,115 total immigrants came to the United States and 550,460 of these were Italians. That means that 11.8 percent of the immigrants over the ten-year period were from Italy. A little over half of the Italians made their homes in the city. When looking into the Italian immigrants of the 1920s, one can easily gain a broad perspective on the overall immigrant experience. The Italians, like the other immigrants, faced prejudice, had different cultural norms, and kept to themselves during the early years of their time in the U.S. Furthermore, just like other ethnic groups, the Italian immigrants eventually assimilated into American culture.

The Italians, like other immigrant groups, faced many hardships when arriving in the United States caused by heavy racism and Nativism. The homeland Americans were not used to the immigrants and for this reason, they thought less of them and oppressed them. The Italians and other immigrants were blamed for many of the nation's problems. For example, the government led raids on immigrants' houses because they feared the immigrants were communists. This was made evident in the Sacco and Vanzetti trial, when two Italian immigrants were convicted for murder although the prosecution had no real substantial evidence. They were convicted mainly because of their beliefs, not their actions. Religious beliefs also brought the immigrants problems. The KKK was openly anti-Catholic and most of the Italians were Catholic.

The immigrants and Italians also contributed to the institution of prohibition. The Americans did not approve of their drinking habits; therefore the prohibition amendment was made for this and other reasons. Job competition was also a major reason for the racist feelings of the Americans. Native white workers saw the immigrants as competitors for the jobs that they felt they should have. A good example of this competition was "birds of passage." These were Italian workers who came to work in the U.S. and later returned to Italy with the money they earned in the U.S. From 1899-1924, 3.8 million Italians came to the United States, but 2.1 million left to return to Italy during the same period. In fact, a May 2, 1920 article in the New York Times, quoting the

Inter-Racial Council, said, "Indiscriminate denunciation of the foreign born in this country is resulting in many leaving America." The Italians received lower pay because of their nationality. The yearly coal miner earnings for Italians during the early 20th century was $286, while for native whites it was $534. As one can see, the Italians, (in comparison with other immigrants), were discriminated against and faced many roadblocks during their early years in the United States.

To curb the rapid movement of immigrants into the United States, the government began to pass a series of laws. The first law passed was the Immigration Act of 1921. This was the first quota law passed by the country to restrict immigration. It restricted immigration to 3 percent of the current population of a specific nationality according to the 1910 census. In 1924, this act was revised and the percentage went down to 2 percent, using the 1890 census. This act further restricted immigration of Italians and other nationalities.

These "Nativist" acts become even more apparent when one looks at the statistics of immigration during these years. Italian immigration into the U.S. in 1907, before the first restriction was enacted, was 222,260. After the amendment of this act in 1924, the immigration of Italians into the U.S. was down to 6,203 in 1925. The acts dealt a vicious blow to the number of foreigners coming to the United States; the pattern can also be seen in the overall immigration, not just with Italians. The country that was founded on immigration was now restricting foreigners from their lands to prevent change in its society.

Italians also followed the assimilation patterns of many of the other ethnic groups. After prolonged exposure to each other, the Italians and Americans became accustomed to the cultures and beliefs of one another. The Americans began to realize that the Italians posed no real threat to them and their society. Interaction between the two races began the incorporation of the Italians into American society. There are two case studies from the book, <u>The Urban Experience of Italian Americans,</u> which show this assimilation process. The first is by Maxine Seller and focuses on the Italian theater of San Francisco during the period from 1905-1925. She found that in the early stages of Italian existence in San Francisco, the Italian immigrants set up and attended theatres of their own language. This continued for about 15 years when these theatres lost their popularity among their usual Italian followers. Sellers found this was due to more Italians going to American theatres. She wrote, "Time, affluence, and Americanization were dissolving the original North Beach community that had supported popular Italian theatre." (61) Another case study on assimilation, by Harry Jebsen Jr., is titled "Assimilation In a Working Class Suburb: The Italians of Blue Island, Illinois." The Italians of Blue Island began in their own community and stayed by themselves. They did not participate much in the American community. Eventually, just as in San Francisco, they began to break out into the American society, and finally became almost completely assimilated. One American from Blue Island said,

> "You can assure the people that Blue Islanders of Italian decent favor an Americanization program… We, ourselves, have accomplished a great deal toward Americanization. You would have been surprised if you could have seen the number of Italians who voted at

the last election. Practically every Italian of
mature years has become a citizen."

This was also the process with other immigrants.
Americanization became common once the immigrants and
Americans became accustomed to each others' cultures.

The Italian experience in the United States represented
the overall immigrant experience during the early 1900s.
The Italians had a wide range of settlement and were
large in number. They faced the hardships, racism, and
discrimination, as did the other immigrants of the 1920s.
Although their travel to the U.S. became heavily restricted,
they still cemented themselves into American culture. They
assimilated into American communities and found their
niche.

Italians also became active in trade unions and produced
several leaders such as Arthuro Giovannitti and Carlo Tresca.
Second-generation Italians became important figures in
progressive politics. This included figures such as Fiorello
LaGuardia, Vito Marcantonio, and Emmanuel Celler. Italians
played an important role in the development of modern
science as well. This included Enrico Fermi, Emilio Segre,
Salvador Luria, Renato Dulbecco and Rita Levimontalcini.

The Italians were only one group of many that emigrated
from their homeland to the United States in search of a better
life. A survey in 1978 revealed that over 5,294,000 people
had immigrated to the United States from Italy in 1920. This
amounted to 10.9 percent of the total foreign immigration
during this period. Though they faced poverty, discrimination
and the isolation of being in a strange land, the Italian people
stuck together. Italian food is a staple in the American diet.
The flood of Italian immigrants in the late nineteenth century

and early twentieth century did not provide the immigrants with simply a better life, it provided the U.S. with another ingredient to add to its melting pot.

"No Irish Need Apply"
The Struggle From Ireland to America
1840-1850s
by Kara Hardie

The struggle of the Irish immigrants to America is one of astounding proportions. Not only did Irish immigrants face discrimination, horrible living conditions and a poor quality of life in Ireland, but also in America, the country they had sought as refuge from the nightmare that was their reality. I am inclined to believe, however, that the restriction and discrimination faced by the Irish from the Americans was not wrong. Instead, a proper response to the invasion of a foreign group of people, in fact, from a country engulfed in disease, starvation, and dictatorship. The circumstances in Ireland were certainly of an extreme nature and the United States did foster hundreds of thousands of fleeing immigrants and provide them with countless opportunities that were unimaginable in their previous situations. Therefore it can be asserted that <u>Irish immigrants were given more than their fair share of opportunities and freedoms considering the endangerment faced by both the American economy and the health and welfare of its citizens.</u>

To fully comprehend the need for the Irish citizens to flee their country, one must understand the conditions they experienced in Ireland during 1840-1850. This was the time of the Great Potato Famine. One of the most unbelievable and devastating events in world history, The Famine dwarfs such other catastrophes as the Great Depression and the present day starvations in Ethiopia and other Third World countries. This is because the Great Potato Famine was the main cause of a mass exodus of over a million Irish citizens in the 1840s and the root of so many other political and economic disasters, unlike any other country has ever seen. There is no certain theory as to how the potato famine began, but many scientists speculate that an over-drowning of potato spuds created a poor harvest which led to no food for any of the country's citizens. Potatoes were the main "cash crop" in Ireland and many farmers relied on potato farming to sustain their income. Many citizens relied on potatoes as a main source of nutrients and sustenance at an inexpensive price. When potatoes were not able to be grown and harvested, hundreds of thousands starved. Matters were only made worse because citizens did not receive any help or support from the Irish government, nor the rich and powerful British government. An estimated one and a half million Irish died during the great famine. It is also estimated that more than half a million people died from disease during the famine years. Over half a million people also lost their homes during this time and eventually died of starvation, disease, or exposure to the elements. A majority of the dead were children. In addition to the great numbers that died, many more fled their homeland in search of better living conditions and hope for themselves and their families. America seemed one of the most promising possibilities. Canada was also a haven for many Irish fleeing their nightmare.

The ships that carried these immigrants to the "promised land" were almost always overcrowded and did not have adequate food and water to maintain life for more then a few weeks. Journeys across the Atlantic took a few months and were often plagued by disease. These dangerous ships and voyages became known as "coffin boats". Often these boats did not complete the voyage to their final destination because of overcrowding, fire on board, icebergs, and the treacherous winter months that were often traveled in desperation. There were no sanitary facilities onboard and it is believed that over five thousand Irish died on the way to other countries. The Irish were often scammed due to the fact that many voyages were rarely monitored and immigrants were denied the food and water promised with the price of their tickets. Another major concern for those on board was the spread of the deadly disease, typhus. It spread through lice and other fetal bacterium and was easily spread in the close quarters that many passengers were forced to endure. Although the conditions were often unbearable on these long, strenuous voyages, many Irish found it a small price to pay for the freedom and wealth they sought in America.

The sudden flow of immigrants to the United States forced the government to take action. The amount of Irish immigrants who were permitted entrance into the land of the free had to be strictly regulated to prevent overpopulation and significant economic downsizing. Therefore, American governments, along with the British, enacted various Passenger Acts, designed to regulate the shipping trade and to protect passengers. The acts, however, were difficult to enforce, especially in small harbors that lacked government supervision. Greedy ship captains and owners did all they could to exploit their passengers; increasing prices while at the same time overcrowding ships to the brim. The Passenger Acts required that there be no more than two people for every five tons of the registered vessels' tonnage. While the acts were aimed at making travel safer, they raised fares, forcing impoverished Irish citizens to scrounge for the money they didn't have to escape their horrible conditions. While

America's intentions were to regulate the number of Irish who were allowed into the country, it was almost impossible to enforce because of the extreme measures that were taken to leave Ireland.

When Irish immigrants finally arrived in America, they experienced significant amounts of discrimination and hardship that they were not anticipating. It was a pathetic, but understandable situation; as long as the Irish stayed in Ireland, the Americans seemed sympathetic: they organized relief plans and sent food, clothing, and money overseas. However, once they landed in America the sympathetic feelings disappeared and discrimination ensued. Americans feared the Irish who were destitute, emaciated, and too weakened from their journey to work. Diseases such as typhus and other such infections were also cause for concern for American citizens. They feared newcomers would take jobs away and drag down wages and as a result, many employers refused to hire Irish. They put signs on their windows that read "NINA," meaning "no Irish need apply." Inspecting officers also refused ships whose passengers were too sick and weak to work. These preventive measures did not stop the hard-working Irish, however. Soon they formed a large percentage of the American labor force. They worked at the lowest jobs, digging canals, railways, and roads. They worked in factories, mills, and coal mines. For their days of hard work, they received the lowest of wages, often a mere 50 cents per day. Most of the Irish immigrants feared farming again and settled in cities. The United States was undergoing a period of Industrial Revolution at the time which fit their working aspirations in urban settings. They also experienced religious discrimination in the United States because many Americans feared Irish Catholics would multiply, overrun the country, and take orders from the Catholic pope in Rome instead of the American president. Despite obstacles that threatened their livelihoods, the Irish remembered the terrible conditions they had escaped and vowed to succeed in their new homes, no matter what the cost.

In conclusion, while the United States allowed these immigrants to pass within its borders, they were by no means welcomed as true citizens of America. Fear and ignorance played a significant role in the discrimination faced by many Irish upon their arrival. Americans feared their jobs would be taken and that they would acquire fatal diseases, to name a few of the concerns. It was a privilege for the Irish to be accepted into America and escape the dreadful conditions they were experiencing in Ireland. The discrimination they were initially presented with was something they had to accept and honor upon realizing that they were imposing themselves in the American citizen's way of life.

Swedish Immigration
by Kristina Butler

"Here is not a nation, but a teeming Nation of nations," observed poet Walt Whitman in regard to the great influx of immigrants into the United States.127 During the 19th and 20th centuries, over twelve million people left their families, possessions, and homelands behind them, fearlessly bound for the golden streets and endless opportunities they believed existed in America. Out of these 12 million immigrants, 1.2 million of them were Swedes. This small group of immigrants was uniquely prepared to settle and tame the wild Midwest, spreading predominantly across what are now Minnesota, Wisconsin, Illinois, North Dakota, and Kansas.

Although the Swedish immigrants who settled here are almost directly responsible for paving the Nation's westward road, and have made numerous contributions to the country, they were one of the only immigrant groups to be completely ignored by the American government. Perhaps it was because the Swedes tended to settle rural areas, or because they were usually quiet and never created any noticeable problems, but the U.S. government took hardly any interest in the Swedes. Swedish immigration to the United States is characterized by high independence on their part and utter indifference on the part of the American government.

Though some Swedes immigrated as early as the 1600s, the largest waves of Swedish immigrants came between 1850 and 1930,128 reaching a peak of about 65,000 immigrants in 1882.129 The Swedes who immigrated to America came for several reasons. Some sought religious freedom from the

Lutheran church, which Swedes were born into and could leave only through formal petition.130 Many young men emigrated to avoid military conscription. At the time, all Swedish males were required to serve a short term in the military, and many youths viewed this as an infringement on their personal rights.131 Others left because they had become upset with Sweden's social structure. The Riksdag, a kind of ruling oligarchy, gave all of the nation's power to the nobles, clergy members, merchants, and landowners, leaving the poor with absolutely no political influence and creating a huge amount of dissatisfaction in the working class.132 The biggest reason, however, for Swedish emigration was Sweden's growing population and worsening economic situation. Sweden's low mortality rate, combined with better living conditions and healthcare, as well as long periods without warfare, created a boom in the country's population growth. Between 1800 and 1910, the population in Sweden swelled from 2.3 million to 5.5 million people.133

By the 1840s, Sweden was already running out of arable land when long periods of alternating torrential rains and droughts struck, creating a devastating famine. Esasias Tegner, a famous Swedish poet of the time, asked, "Is it true what so many say that the day darkens for old Europe? For to the West beyond the sea, where the sun sets for us, there does it rise for a happier world. There Europe has already sent many of her best hopes."134 America, with its vast amounts of farmland, new employment opportunities from the industrial revolution, and chance at a new life, seemed extremely enticing to many poor Swedes who were oppressed by the problems in their homeland.

The Swedes, however, were somewhat misguided in their vision of America. The very first immigrants who ventured to this country began a tradition, which continued over the years, of writing letters home to Sweden. These letters, though, were almost always full of praise and enthusiasm, neglecting to write about America honestly, and preferring to exaggerate its positive traits. For that reason, many Swedes immigrated thinking they would find a paradise, where the farmland had no stones, and where they would never have to obey anyone but themselves.135

After a 10 month-long voyage on a cargo ship, Swedish immigrants arrived at America's shores hungry, tired, and sick. They then usually had another long journey to reach wherever their final destination was located. Many were disappointed when they found out that the "land of dreams" wasn't exactly as they had imagined, but most Swedish immigrants remained positive. Hans Mattson had this to say, "At that time America was little known in our part of the country, only a few persons having emigrated from the whole district. But we knew that it was a new country inhabited by a free and independent people, that it had a liberal government and great natural resources, and these inducements were enough."136

Swedish immigrants arrived with perfect skills to take advantage of the nation's move westward. Coming from Sweden, a northern country full of mountains and lakes, they were adept at logging, mining, fishing, and construction,137 all necessary skills for the rough work involved in settling the Midwest. Moreover, the American government had passed the Homestead Act in 1862, promising 160 acres of land to anyone who agreed to settle it for more than five years.138 The Swedish immigrants quickly became the workforce that pioneered and settled the United States' heartland. During the great immigration period, Swedish immigrants cleared over 10 million acres of land, 2 million of which were in Minnesota alone.139 They lived in tents or dugouts until they had time to build a log cabin, one of the uniquely Swedish contributions to American heritage.

Swedish immigrants also helped build the nation's railroads. The Rock Island Line, which ran through Illinois, and the Northern Pacific Line, which ran through Minnesota and North Dakota, were mostly built by Swedes.140 Although most Swedish immigrants tended to settle the American Midwest, many also settled cites, such as Chicago, and even in parts of Canada. Throughout this time, however, the U.S. government played hardly any role at all in the lives of Swedish American settlers.

The Swedes were a highly independent, self-sufficient, and somewhat isolated group of settlers. They paid little attention to the political, social, and economic conditions of the country, choosing instead to settle in rural areas and to keep to themselves. They found jobs, set up their own churches and schools, and kept their language and traditions alive by forming tight-knit Swedish communities. Men generally acquired jobs working for the railroad or for lumber companies, and when those jobs were finished they worked on building the family farm. It was a hard labor lifestyle, and was oftentimes dangerous. Aviator Charles Lindberg recounts his grandfather's accident as a logger, "One day he stumbled, and fell against the spinning saw. Its teeth cut through his arm near the shoulder and ripped open his back…The mill hands claimed that his gash was so deep they could see my grandfather's heart beating."141

Women who came to America on their own found jobs as domestic servants or as dressmakers. Those who came to the new land with a family usually worked at home and on the farm. Swedish women thought themselves lucky to be in a place with so many job opportunities. In a letter from 1871, Stina Wiback writes, "A woman here can support herself and her husband rather well on her earning, without his earning anything, for that is what I have been doing ever since I came here."142

Since the government did not do much to ensure education to Swedish immigrants, the Swedes took it upon themselves to set up their own schools. Schools were originally designed so that immigrant children would not forget the language and history of their homeland. Churches and parents took the initiative to create schools and most classes were taught in Swedish. This, however, changed several years later, as Swedes began to learn that it was difficult to assimilate into American culture by teaching their children's classes in Swedish. During that time, many church-related colleges and seminaries were also created by the Swedish immigrants. Examples of these institutions include, Bethany College, Augustana College, Gustavus Adolphus College, and Upsala College.143 From about 1910 to 1917, high schools in the Midwest actually offered courses in Scandinavian languages, but they were cut due to a lack of funding once the U.S. entered the First World War.144

In addition to creating schools, Swedish immigrants also funded services such as hospitals, orphanages, and homes for the elderly. Many of the immigrants' lives were centered around the church and the community, one of the reasons why they have held on to their traditions so long after emigrating. Church services were conducted in Swedish for many years and the first generation of Swedes in America actually sent back to Sweden for Lutheran ministers to come lead their services.145

Swedes also found ways to help each other through the immigration process. Brothers Olaf and Jonas Hedstrom were robbed when they first reached America and after that worked hard to set up a Bethel Mission that would help Swedish immigrants avoid port dangers and make a safe journey to their destination. After their idea took off, many other Bethel Missions emerged, all designed to make the immigrants' passage a little less difficult. Because the Swedes existed in such community-based groups, and were living mostly in rural areas, it took them longer as a people to assimilate into American culture. Even though they were slow to assimilate, the U.S. government paid no attention to them at all.

In their first years in America, Swedish immigrants had no real desire to get involved in politics. Many Swedes fought in the Civil War and in World War I, even though they had trouble fighting against their old neighbor, Germany; the laws that were being passed in Congress, however, seemed too far away to be of any importance to them. Swedish immigrants had always been partial to the Republican Party because they liked its anti-slavery platform, its idea of giving land away to new settlers, and its slogan, "a nation of free men, free homes, and free work."146 The Republicans, however, took advantage of this, tossing the Swedes aside as "voting cattle," or a guaranteed vote, and never repaying them for their support. In fact, up until 1900 only a few Swedes had ever held a political office.147

The Swedes, however, had a perfect opportunity for political influence in Minnesota, where they made up 15 percent of the total population. Combined with other Scandinavian groups, especially Norway, they amounted to 30 percent of Minnesota's total population, making

Scandinavians the largest immigrant group and Germans the second largest.148 Because of this, both the Republicans and the Democrats were forced to support Scandinavian candidates in order to earn Scandinavian support in the Midwest.149

Though political parties had to take an interest in the Swedes, the national government remained indifferent towards them. Swedish immigration expert Sten Carlsson noted the same thing, "...However, in its relations with Sweden, the American government is not obliged to take any appreciable consideration to Swedish Americans on the whole or to Swedish-American politicians."150 The fact that the U.S. government never took any interest in the Swedish immigrants was not a bad thing, nor was it in any way mean-spirited. The Swedes simply never produced a reason for the government to become involved in their lives.

There is no set American response to Swedish immigration. As with all the immigrant groups, Americans viewed the Swedes with mixed feelings. Many Americans who had been here long before the Swedes were critical. They stereotyped Swedish immigrants as stupid or snobbish, because most of the Swedes had blond hair and had a tendency to be quiet. The quiet Swedes, however, also gained respect in the eyes of Americans for their hard work and incredible strength of character. Journalist Paul Hosmer noticed this extreme work ethic, saying,

> "For some reason every Swede heads for the lumbering centers as soon as he arrives in this country and he is a fixture around lumber camps and sawmills. He knows no English, has no money, can neither read, write, nor talk so anyone can understand him...In 30

days he can ask for snuff and 15 different kinds of food in English, he has made more money out of his contract than six American laborers working beside him..."151

As the years progressed, more and more Swedes emerged as important political and intellectual figures, as well as important athletes and entertainers, and Swedish-Americans finally broke any stereotypes they had formally been held to.

Out of the total number of immigrants who came to America during the 19th and 20th centuries, the Swedes made-up only a small percentage. For such a small group of people, however, Swedish immigrants have made numerous contributions. Despite this, they were never really noticed by the American government. During their early years here, the Swedes were highly independent and self-sufficient. They tamed the Midwest, worked hard at their jobs, created their own schools, and lived in their own communities, never needing or wanting any help from the U.S. government. As can be seen, the Swedish immigrant experience in America was characterized by high independence and governmental indifference.

HOW THE WEST WAS LOST
by Ahren Freund, Philip John, Kimberly Wagner

An undesirable massive population explosion is upon us, thanks to illegal immigration and declining birthrates of the current citizenry. These harmful effects place huge burdens on our nation's infrastructure. Schools, hospitals, and social services simply cannot keep up with a huge increase in the number of poor people, who now play the largest role in our increasing population. These issues are immigration and dwindling populations. Immigrant invasions and dying populations imperil our country and civilization.

Economically, socially, culturally, and ethnically we are becoming a nation of many different cultures that have little in common with one another. For example, we are definitely affected by the poverty in Mexico. Many Mexicans come into our country illegally and we end up subsidizing their living here through our taxes. Additionally, we cannot sustain our standard of living if we continue to harbor so many illegal immigrants, without doing major damage to the environment. All of the gains in clean air and emissions controls in California are being wiped out by such a huge increase in the population of poor people (immigrants) who cannot afford tune-ups for their cars.

Most Mexican immigrants do not acknowledge the sovereignty of the United States nor do they want to assimilate into our society. They would rather live in Mexico. This is a huge departure from the past, when people immigrated here legally and they wanted to become part of America. It was a commitment on their part. Their home countries were far away, but those days are gone. In Santa Ana, California, where three quarters of the residents are Latino, less than a quarter of the municipal library's books are in Spanish and residents would like to see that number go up. This is an example of how immigrants are not assimilating into an English speaking country.

As Christianity becomes a dying faith in every Western nation, every Western nation is becoming irrevocably changed. Not one Western nation has a native-born population that is replenishing itself. Before the end of the century, at present birth rates, all Western nations' native-born populations will be overrun by other cultures.

A correlation has been proven between strong religious faith and larger family size. The Christian population began to die out because Western people began to have fewer children. The less devout a people, whether Christian, Muslim, or Jewish, the lower its birthrate will be and the more devout a people, the higher its birthrate will be. People in the Western nations are not as devout about their faith as those in other nations. In other nations, the religions strongly encourage large families and limited birth control.

In addition to declining birthrates, illegal immigration plays a large role in the collapse of Western society. As immigrants come into Western countries, they begin to establish themselves with their high birthrates and because of this they slowly begin to take over the culture and the country. Not to say that immigration is always a bad thing, because many come with good intentions to better themselves in a Western society and to improve the society in which they reside. The immigrants who come to harm the society, not to fit in, or even to create violence are the ones we are against.

"In the 1950s President Eisenhower sent illegal aliens packing in Operation Wetback and apologized to no one for defending U.S. borders and ordering intruders to go home." (Buchanan, 208) Neither Democrats nor Republicans today any longer demand that we seal a border that hundreds of thousands of aliens attempt to cross every year. When members of the House and Senate have been asked if they support the deportation of illegal aliens who get into the country, only a small fraction would say, "Yes." Many Hispanic-Americans would probably not vote for members of Congress who demand that our immigration laws be enforced and since Hispanic-Americans have an increasing number of votes, Congress will not insist that the President enforce them. America is losing a cultural war. Separatism is triumphing over integration. The melting pot has become a salad bowl, and the impact upon American society, politics and culture is devastating.

The largest population movement in history is coming from places like Mexico, Asia, Africa, and Latin America and most are not coming with the intentions of fitting in.

> "In 1960 only 16 million Americans did not trace their ancestors to Western Europe. Today 80 million do not. Largely because of immigration, there is no majority race in Hawaii, Houston, or New York City. Within five years there will be no majority race in our largest state, California. No other nation in history has undergone a demographic change of this magnitude in so short a time. No nation in history has gone through a demographic change in this short a time, and remained the same nation." (Buchanan, 3)

117

Uncontrolled immigration threatens to destroy the nation we grew up in and convert America into a society of people with almost nothing in common; not history, heroes, language, culture, faith, or ancestors. As mentioned before we are becoming more like a salad bowl rather than a melting pot, because new peoples are not melting together and forming one people.

Millions have begun to feel like strangers in their own land. They see the art and artifacts of their past being removed from their museums only to be replaced by depressing, ugly, abstract, anti-American art and artifacts. They watch as books that they treasured disappear from the schools they attended only to be replaced by books whose authors they have never heard of. The moral code that they were raised to live by is becoming non-existent. The culture they grew up with is dying inside of their own country. In their lifetime many Americans have had their heroes devalued, their culture polluted, their values questioned, the principles upon which their country was founded attacked, and they themselves held up to ridicule as extremists and bigots for holding on to beliefs that they have held for generations. Our world is being turned upside down - what was right and true yesterday is wrong and false today.

Strong proponents for immigrant rights testify to the negative impact mass immigration has on this country. In an article titled "Rethinking Immigration Policy" from the January 31, 1995 San Francisco Chronicle, Yeh Ling-Ling, National Outreach Coordinator for the Carrying Capacity Network, cites several leading immigration rights' advocates views on immigration. Below are several of the responses to the editor provided in the article.

Chinese American Professor Paul Ong of UCLA said, "In terms of the adverse impact (of immigration) on wages and employment, the adverse impact will be most pronounced on minorities and established immigrants."

Antonia Hernandez, the president of the Mexican American Legal Defense and Educational Fund, said, "Migration, legal and undocumented, does have an impact on our economy... Most of the competition is to the Latino community. We compete with each other for those low-paying jobs."

The pro-immigration Urban Institute indicated: "Less-skilled black workers and black workers in high immigration areas with stagnant economies are negatively affected (by immigration)..."

Bill Ong Hing, a Stanford University law professor said: "There's a certain legitimacy to the view that parts of the country are being overcrowded with immigrants.... They affect growth, air pollution, and water availability. It's not bogus for people to raise that issue."

These quotes serve to verify what Patrick J. Buchanan writes about in his book, <u>The Death of the West</u>. Buchanan repeats numerous times in his book the theme expressed in the following quotes that the Western world is dying.

> As a growing population has long been a mark of healthy nations and rising civilizations, falling populations have been a sign of nations and civilizations in decline. If that holds true, Western civilization, power and wealth aside, is in critical condition. For, like the Cheshire Cat, the people of the West have begun to fade away." (Buchanan, 11)

In 1960, people of European ancestry were one-fourth of the world's population; in 2000, they were one-sixth; in 2050, they will be one-tenth. These are the statistics of a vanishing race. A growing awareness of what they portend has induced a sense of foreboding, even panic, in Europe. (Buchanan, 12)

America is not invincible to the powers of separatism. America is overflowing with immigrants. Immigrants are taking over the institutions that shape and transmit ideas, opinions, beliefs, and values found in television, the arts, entertainment, and education. This is creating a whole new America. Not just ethnically and racially, but culturally and morally as well. We are no longer "one nation under God."

The United States is a nation of immigrants. We have millions of poor in this country, composed disproportionately of minorities. Our millions of unemployed are mostly low-skilled, mostly non-white. Even if immigrants are high achievers should we invest in our own citizens or in citizens of other countries?

The United States may still have millions of acres of open space, but the land area alone, however, cannot support human lives. Newcomers need water, food, as well as jobs, education, healthcare, welfare, and other services that we cannot even provide to millions of our native-born Americans.

We are paving and building over some of the most productive agricultural land in the world as cities move out from their centers. In addition, massive urban crowding is beginning to take its toll on inner city and even suburban living standards because immigrants pack several families in one household thus lowering property values in these cities.

We must bear in mind that today's global economy depends on fewer but highly skilled workers to prosper. The United States does not even have the resources to prepare today's children to be tomorrow's productive workers. Where are we going to find tax dollars to educate the additional thousands of immigrant children coming to our country every year?

Replaced is the good country we grew up in with a wasteland that is not worth living in and not worth fighting for. Their country, not ours.

> "Between 2000 and 2050, world population will grow by more than three billion to over 9 billion, but this 50 percent increase in global population will come entirely in Asia, Africa, and Latin America, as one hundred million people of European descent vanish from the Earth. There are 30 million foreign born citizens in the U.S. and between 9 and 11 million illegal aliens. That is as many illegal immigrants as there are people in Massachusetts, Rhode Island and Connecticut combined." (Buchanan, 54)

Societies that organized to ensure the maximum pleasure, freedom, and happiness for all their members are at the same time advancing the date of their own funerals. Fate may compensate the Mexican, Asian, Islamic, and Latin peoples for their hardships and poverty in this century with the domination of the Earth in the next. Do we not have it on high authority that, "Blessed are the meek…. they shall inherit the Earth." (Matthew 5:5)

Probably the most devastating effect of illegal immigration is the fact that increased job competition depresses wages for vulnerable American workers and the next wave of immigrants. This then lowers their opportunities to get ahead in life and their ability to support their families. This creates a permanent lower class, the likes of which can be seen in any Third World Country and creates a society of haves and have-nots.

In *USA Today*, May 19, 2003, Rick Hampson writes about Anaheim, CA and how the influx of immigrants has greatly changed the nature of the community. Today Anaheim is about half Latino, a tenth Asian and about a third Anglo. Its people speak more than 60 languages, and one study concluded that the city has more integrated and diverse neighborhoods than Los Angeles. One resident said, "You just get used to everybody being different than you. Some people don't like it, but I do."

Is this what it's going to come to? We just have to give up and get used to everyone being different from everyone else? The United States needs a time out from immigration to rethink its immigration policy that is not only faulty but also economically foolish and environmentally harmful.

Bibliography

Adugna, Gabeyehu. "African Immigration in the Modern Era." 5/5/98. 2004.<raven.umd.edu/~mddlmddl/791/communities/html/africanmd.html>.

Diverse Strategies. 2003. 2004.<www.ethnicmajority.com/immigration.htm>.

Buchanan, Patrick J. The Death of the West. New York, New York: St. Martin's Press, 2002.

Fox, Geoffrey. Culture, Politics, and the Constructing of Identity Hispanic Nation. Secaucus, New Jersey: Carol Publishing Group, 1996.

Galvan, Raul. Cultures of America Cuban American. New Bellmore, New York: Marshall Cavendish Corp., 1995.

Gonzalez-Pando, Miguel. The Cuban Americans. Westport, Connecticut: Greenwood Press, 1998.

Mendez, Adriana. Cubans in America. Minneapolis: Lerner Publications Company, 1994.

Olson, James and Judith. Cuban Americans From Trauma to Triumph. New York, New York: Twayne Publishers, 1995.

Hoobler, Dorothy and Thomas. <u>The Cuban American Family Album.</u> New York, New York: Oxford University Press, 1996.

Fariello, Griffin. <u>Red Scare: Memories of the American Inquisition</u>. W.W. Norton & Co.: New York, 1995.

Dolan, Sean. <u>The Polish Americans</u>. Chelsea House Publishers: New York, 1997.

Gabor, Al. <u>Polish Americans</u>. Marshall Cavendish Corporation: New York, 1995.

Galicich, Anne. <u>The German Americans</u>. Chelsea House Publishers: USA, 1989.

Lee, Jan. "John Louis von Neumann." 9 Feb. 2002: On-line. 31 Oct. 2003. Available <http://ei.cs.vt.edu/~history/ VonNeumann.html>.

Toor, Rachel. <u>The Polish Americans</u>. Chelsea House Publishers: Singapore, 1995.

Fariello, Griffin. <u>Red Scare: Memories of the American Inquisition</u>. W.W. Norton &
Co.: New York, 1995.

Dolan, Sean. <u>The Polish Americans</u>. Chelsea House Publishers: New York, 1997.

Gabor, Al. <u>Polish Americans</u>. Marshall Cavendish Corporation: New York, 1995.

Galicich, Anne. The German Americans. Chelsea House Publishers: USA, 1989.

Toor, Rachel. The Polish Americans. Chelsea House Publishers: Singapore, 1995.

Mayberry, Jodine. Eastern Europeans. New York: Franklin Watts, 1991, p.35, 37, 39-41.

Papp, Susan. Hungarian Americans and Their Communities of Cleveland. New York: Orchard Books, 2001, p. 79, 80, 81.

Portes, Alejandro. Immigrant America: A Portrait. Berkeley: University of California Press, 1990, p.31, 32, 34, 160.

Press, Petra. A Multicultural Portrait of Immigration. New York: Benchmark Books, 1996, p. 15, 29, 36.

Rhatican, Bill. "American Policy on Refugees: Was It Driven By The Cold War?" July 19, 2001, pg. 9, 10, 11, 12.

Litton, Helen, The Irish Famine; An Illustrated History, Wolfhound Press Ltd., Dublin, Ireland, 1994.

Woodham-Smith, Cecil, The Great Hunger, Ireland 1845-1849, Penguin Books, London, England, 1991.

Boyer, Clark, et.al. <u>The Enduring Vision</u>: <u>A History of the American People</u> (5th Edition). Houghton Mifflin Company: New York, NY. 2004.

Rhatican, William F. "The Irish Immigrant of the 1850s. A Help or Hindrance to His Immigrant Successors?"

<u>The Irish in America</u> .Terry Golway. Video. Disney Enterprises Inc. 1997.

Woodham-Smith, Cecil, <u>The Great Hunger; Ireland 1845-1849,</u> Penguin Books, London, England, 1991.

Dezell, Maureen. <u>Irish America: Coming Into Clover</u>. New York, NY, 2000

Deignan, Tom. <u>Irish Americans</u>. Hauppauge, NY, 2002

"Encyclopedia: Philadelphia Nativist Riots." <u>Nationmaster. com</u>. 11/2003.
<<u>http://www.nationmaster.com/encyclopedia/ Philadelphia-Nativist-Riots</u>>

Miller, Kerby A. <u>Emigrants and Exiles</u>. New York, NY, 1985

Sage, Henry J. "Expansion and Manifest Destiny:America in the 1840s". 2003.
<<u>http://www.nv.cc.va.us/home/nvsageh/Hist121/ Part4/1840s.html</u>.>

Hutchmacher, Joseph. <u>A Nation of Newcomers</u>. New York: Delacorte Press, 1967.

Rolle, Andrew. <u>The Immigrant Upraised</u>. Oklahoma: University of Oklahoma Press, 1960.

Denver, Barbara. Interview.

Di Stasi, Lawrence. <u>The Big Book of Italian Culture</u>. New York: Penmen Inc., 1991.

Bailey, Thomas and Kennedy, David. <u>The American Pageant</u>. Massachusetts: D.C. Heath and Company, 1991.

<u>Italians Gale Encyclopedia of Multicultural America</u>. Boston: Gale Research, Inc., 1995.

Wyhte, Robert."The Journey of an Irish Coffin Ship 1847". 1998. 2003. <<u>http://www.people.virginia.edu/~eas5e/Irish/ RWhyte.html</u>.>

"In Search of Freedom." <u>Cappelen.No</u>. 2003. <<u>http://www. cappelen.no/fp-cuv/passageny/insearch.htm</u>

Lee, Jonathan and Robert Siemborski. <u>The American Immigration Home Page</u>. 2000. <<u>http://www.bergen. org/AAST/Projects/Immigration/</u>.>

"Fearful Facts" and "Hunger, Cold, Disease and Deaths." The Wexford Independent. 1846. <u>Liz Szabo's Home Page.</u> 2003.

Edited by Bill Rhatican

<http://www.people.virginia.edu/~eas5e/.>

Potter, George W. *To the Golden Door; the Story of the Irish in Ireland and America.* Boston: Little, Brown, 1960.

Pencak, William, Selma Berrol, and Randall Miller. *Immigration to New York.* Philadephia: Balch Institute Press, 1991.

Byrne, Stephen. *Irish Immigration to the United States.* New York: Arno Press, 1969.

Ernst, Robert. *Immigrant Life in New York City, 1825-1863.* New York: King's Crown Press, 1949.

Bennett, William. *Narrative of a Recent Journey of Six Weeks in Ireland.* London: C. Gilpin, 1847, pp. 25-9.

Barone, Michael "Attention: Congress Acting Sensibly." *U.S. News and World Report*, March 20, 1995, p. 44.

Bornemeir, James. "Feinstein Introduces Measure to Cope with Illegal Immigration." *Washington Post*, March 22, 1995.

Buchanan, Patrick J. *The Death of the West. How Dying Populations and Immigrant Invasions Imperil Our Country and Civilization.* New York, NY: St. Martin's Press, 2002.

Congressional Immigration Reform. Immigration Laws: April 1995- Number 3. 17 March 2003. <u>Australia Visa.</u>
<<u>http://migrationint.com.au/news/andorra/apr_ 1995-03.html</u>.>

Hampson, Rick "'New Brooklyns' Replace White Suburbs." *USA Today*, May 16, 2003.

Ling-Ling, Yeh. "Rethinking Immigration Policy." *San Francisco Chronicle* Op-Ed. January 31, 1995.

Lacey, Mark. "New Task Force Targets Illegal Immigration." *Los Angeles Times*, March 16, 1995.

Moore, Michael. *Stupid White Men and Other Sorry Excuses for the State of a Nation.* New York, NY: Harper Collins, 2001.

About the Author

An interesting series of essays on immigration written by 37 advanced placement U.S. government seniors in an ethnically diverse public high school in Northern Virginia. Many of these perspectives are by students who are either immigrants themselves or are descendants of earlier immigrants. Their views range from left to right; From "open the gates to all" to the "pull up the drawbridge" mentality of Pat Buchanan.

(Footnotes)

[1] Hoobler, Dorothy, Thomas, <u>The Cuban American Family Album,</u> New York, New York, 1996, pg. 56.

[2] Mendez, Adriana, <u>Cubans in America,</u> Minneapolis, 1994, pg. 37.

[3] Gonzalez-Pando, Miguel, <u>The Cuban Americans,</u> Westport, Connecticut, 1998, pg. 35.

[4]Mendez, pg. 38.

[5] Galvan, Raul, <u>Cultures of America: Cuban Americans,</u> New Bellmore, New York, 1995, pg. 18.

[6] Mendez, pg. 51.

[7] Gonzalez-Pando, pg. 53.

[8] Olson, James, Judith, <u>Cuban Americans From Trauma to Triumph,</u> New York, New York, 1995, pg. 64.

[9] Gonzalez-Pando, pg. 57.

[1]Schiavo. *Four Centuries of Italian American History.* P. 152

[2]Parini, Ciongoli. *Passage to Liberty.* P. 9

[3]Schiavo.*Four Centuries of Italian-American History.* P. 152

[4]Moreno. *Italian Americans.* P. 28

[5]Gompers. http://www.spartacus.schoolnet.co.uk/USAEitaly.htm

[6]id at P. 29

[7]Schiavo. *Four Centuries of Italian American History.* P. 152

[8]id at P. 37-38

[9]Moreno. *Italian Americans.* P. 45

[10]id at P. 43

[11]id at P. 78

[12]Marks. *Chicago Tribune.* May 17th, 1890. http://www.spartacus.schoolnet.co.uk/USAEitaly.htm

[13]Moreno. *Italian Americans.* P. 55

[14]Pellegrini. http://www.spartacus.schoolnet.co.uk/USAEitaly.htm

[15]Carr. *The Coming of the Italian*(*The Outlook* February 24th, 1906)

[16]Ciongoli, Parini. *Passage to Liberty.* P. 22

[17]Id.

[18]Moreno. *Italian Americans.* P. 43

[19]Marks. *Chicago Tribune,* May 17th 1890 http://www.spartacus.schoolnet.co.uk/USAEitaly.htm

20 Dolan, Sean. <u>The Polish Americans</u>. Chelsea House Publishers: New York, 1997, p. 37.

21 Bender, David L. <u>Immigration: Opposing Viewpoints</u>. Greenharan Press: New York,1998, p. 63.

22Galicich, Anne. <u>The German Americans</u>. Chelsea House Publishers: USA, 1989, p. 40.

23 Galicich, p.42.

24 Dolan, p.38.

25Galicich, p. 42.

26Toor, Rachel. <u>The Polish Americans</u>. Chelsea House Publishers: Singapore, 1995, p. 26.

27Galicich, p. 65.

28Toor, p. 57.

29Fariello, Griffin. <u>Red Scare: Memories of the American Inquisition</u>. W.W. Norton & Co.: New York, 1995, p.18-19.

30Lee, Jan. "John Louis von Neumann." 9 Feb. 2002: n.pag. On-line. Internet. 31 Oct. 2003. Available WWW:http:// http://ei.cs.vt.edu/~history/VonNeumann.html.

31 Galicich, Anne. (1989).The German Americans. p.73. New York: Chelsea House Publishers.

32 Galicich, Anne. (1989).The German Americans. p.77. New York: Chelsea House Publishers.

33 Galicich, Anne. (1989).The German Americans. p.79. New York: Chelsea House Publishers.

34 Roosevelt, Theodore. (1894). What Americanism Is.

35 Wilson, Woodrow. (1915).The State of the Union Address.

36 Galicich, Anne. (1989).The German Americans. p.81. New York: Chelsea House Publishers.

37 Zimmerman, Arthur. (1917). The Zimmerman Telegram.

38 Wagner, Helen. (1972).

[39]Mayberry, Jodine. Eastern Europeans. New York: Franklin Watts, 1991, p.35.

[40]Rhatican, Bill. "American Policy on Refugees: Was It Driven By The Cold War?" July 19, 2001, pg. 9.

[41]Mayberry, p. 35.

[42]Portes, Alejandro. Immigrant America: A Portrait. Berkeley: University of California Press, 1990, p.31.

[43]Ibid, pg. 32.

[44]Mayberry, p. 37.

[45]Portes, p. 34.

[46]Mayberry, p. 39.

[47]Press, Petra. A Multicultural Portrait of Immigration. New York: Benchmark Books, 1996, p. 15.

[48]Mayberry, p. 40.

[49]Rhatican, p. 11.

[50]Press, p. 29.

[51]Rhatican, p. 11.

[52]Portes, p. 160.

[53]Ibid.

[54]Press, p. 36.

[55]Papp, Susan. Hungarian Americans and Their Communities of Cleveland. New York: Orchard Books, 2001, p. 79.

[56]Mayberry, p. 41.

[57]Papp, p. 80.

[58]Ibid, pg. 81.

[59]Rhatican, p. 12.

[60]Ibid, p. 10.

61 Litton, Helen, The Irish Famine; An Illustrated History, Wolfhound Press Ltd., Dublin, Ireland, 1994 P.10

62 Woodham-Smith, Cecil, The Great Hunger, Ireland 1845-1849, Penguin Books, London, England, 1991, p 31.

63 Times (London), February 10, 1846, Lead editorial

64 Boyer, Clark, Kett, Salisbury, Sitkoff, Woloch, <u>The Enduring</u> Vision: <u>A History of the American</u> People (5th Edition). Houghton Mifflin Company, Boston, MA, New York, Ny, 2004. p. 381

65 Boyer, Clark, Kett... p. 275

66 Boyer, Clark, Kett...p. 382

67 Boyer, Clark, Kett...p. 382

68 Boyer, Clark, Kett...p. 383

69 Rhatican, William F., "The Irish Immigrant of the 1850s. A Help or Hindrance to His Immigrant Successors?", p. 7

70 Bill Rhatican Immigration paper, see also Woodham-Smith, Cecil, <u>The Great Hunger; Ireland 1845-1849,</u> Penguin Books, London, England, 1991. First ed. 1962. P. 75.

71 *Irish in America* 1997 Disney enterprises P. 3

72 *Irish in America* Chapter 2

73 *Irish in America* P. 3

74

75

76 *Irish in America* P. 45

77 *Irish in America* political cartoon P. 57

78 *Irish in America* Chapter 3 P. 75

79 *Irish in America* Chapter 3

80 Miller, Kerby A., <u>Immigrants and Exiles</u>, Oxford University Press, New York, NY, 1985. pp 26-28.

81 Rhatican, Bill, <u>AN GORA MOR THE GREAT HUNGER: A LOOK AT THE IRISH FAMINE: 1846 –1851.</u> p. 5.

82 Daniels, Roger, <u>Coming to America, A History of Immigration and Ethnicity in American Life.</u> Harper Perennial. New York, NY, 1990 p. 133.

83 Miller, p. 281.

84 Daniels, p. 128.

85 Daniels, p. 129

86 Coogan, Tim Pat. <u>Wherever Green is Worn.</u> Palgrave Publishing, New York, NY, 2000. p. 253.

87 Leinwald, Gerald, <u>American Immigration: Should the Open Door Be Closed?</u> Franklin Watts, New York, NY, 1995. p. 9.

88 Asbury, Herbert, <u>The Gangs of New York.</u> Thunder's Mouth Press, New York, NY, 1927.

89 Crocker, Richard. <u>http://www.govexec.com/features/0197s4s2.htm</u>.

90 Daniels, p. 136

91 Daniels p. 138

92 Coogan, p. 285.

93 Times (London), February 10, 1846, Lead editorial

94 p. 381

95 Litton, Helen, <u>The Irish Famine; An Illustrated History,</u> Wolfhound Press Ltd., Dublin, Ireland, 1994 P.10

96 Woodham-Smith, Cecil, <u>The Great Hunger, Ireland 1845-1849</u>, Penguin Books, London, England, 1991, p 31.

97 p. 275

98 p. 382

99 p. 382

100 Dezell, Maureen. <u>Irish America: Coming Into Clover</u>. New York, NY, 2000. p. 18

101 Dezell, p. 18

102 Dolan, Jay P. <u>http://migration.ucc.ie/conferences%20and%20publications/conferences/scattering/conferencepapers/Prof.%20Jay%20P.%20Dolan.htm</u>. University of Notre Dame. 1997

103 Dolan. http://migration.ucc.ie...

104 Sage, Henry J. <u>http://www.nv.cc.va.us/home/nvsageh/Hist121/Part4/1840s.html</u>. 1996-2003

105 Sage. http://www.nv.cc.va.us...

106 Miller, Kerby A. <u>Emigrants and Exiles</u>. New York, NY, 1985. p. 319

107 Betty Caroli, Immigrants Who Returned Home (Chelsea House Pub., 1990), 77.

108 David Reimers, The Immigrant Experience (Chelsea House Pub., 1989), 91.

109 Caroli, 78.

110 William Evitts, *Early Immigration in the United States (Library of Congress, 1989), 142.*

111 Evitts, 46.

112 Joseph Hutchmaker, *A Nation of Newcomers* (Delacorte Press, 1967), 51.

113 Caroli, 18.

114 Reimers, 99.

115 Hutchmaker, 120.

116 Reimers, 14.

117 Caroli, 87

118 Allyson McGill, The Swedish Americans, New York, Ny., 1988, p. 7

119 McGill, p. 14

120 Irene Franck, The Scandinavian Heritage, New York, Ny., 1988, p. 72

121 McGill, p. 34

122 McGill, p. 35

123 McGill, p. 34

124 McGill, p. 32

125 McGill, p. 33

126 McGill, p. 37

127 Betty Caroli, Immigrants Who Returned Home, New York, Ny., 1990, p. 39

128 McGill, p. 13

129 Dorothy and Thomas Hoobler, The Scandinavian American Family Album, New York, Ny., 1997, p. 122

130 Franck, p. 72

131 Franck, p. 72

132 Hoobler, p. 48

133 Hoobler, p. 58

134 Franck, pp. 74-75

135 Lars Ljungmark, <u>Swedish Exodus</u>, London, England, 1979, p. 121

136 David Reimers, <u>The Immigrant Experience</u>, New York, Ny., 1989, p. 62

137 Ljungmark, p. 101

138 Ljungmark, p. 101

139 Hans Norman and Harald Runblom (editors), A collective work of the Uppsala Migration Research Project, <u>From Sweden to America: A History of the Migration</u>, Minneapolis, Mn., 1976, p. 291

140 Norman and Runblom, p. 294

141 Norman and Runblom, p. 300

142 Hoobler, p. 52